Contents

Introduction to Vocational Business series

This textbook is one of a series covering the core areas of business studies. The first six books in the series cover the core units of the Business AVCE. A further five books look at the most popular optional units. Each book focuses on vocational aspects of business, rather than theoretical models, allowing the reader to understand how businesses operate. To complement this vocational focus, each book contains a range of case studies illustrating how businesses respond to internal and external changes.

The textbooks are designed to support students taking a range of business courses. While each is free standing, containing the essential knowledge required by the various syllabuses and course requirements, together they provide a comprehensive coverage of the issues facing both large and small businesses in today's competitive environment.

Titles in the series

Book 1	**Business at Work**
Book 2	**The Competitive Business Environment**
Book 3	**Marketing**
Book 4	**Human Resources**
Book 5	**Finance**
Book 6	**Business Planning**

Optional units: **Financial Accounting**
Market Research
Marketing and Promotional Strategy
Business and the European Union
Training, Developing and Motivating People

Introduction

This book is specifically related to optional units for the AVCE Business courses offered by Edexcel, OCR and AQA. In particular:

- Edexcel – Unit 19 Motivating and Developing People (Advanced)
- OCR – Unit 15 Training and Development (7244)
- AQA – Unit 10 Training and Development.

This book can serve the needs of the general business reader with an interest in training, development and motivation. It is written to provide a brief introduction to some of the main terms and concepts associated with training and development and will also help students following introductory professional qualifications in this area.

Training, development and motivation are important tools for business success if changes in technology and working practices are to be used for the benefit of business and employees alike. This book shows you why training and motivation is important and looks at some of the commonly used techniques. It will help you understand how businesses approach the training and motivation process from a practical and theoretical point of view.

Training and development is currently the subject of a great number of government policy initiatives. It is hoped that the many websites referred to in the text will be used by students and teachers alike to keep abreast of the exciting developments that are taking place.

Acknowledgements

Thanks to Jane Cotter at Nelson Thornes for her continued patience and support. Appreciation for Marie, James and Michelle at home for not only putting up with the disruption caused by writing this book but also suggesting some of the quotes at the start of each section. Phil White, as he has been for the last 30 years, was a much appreciated source of materials and comment. Any errors or omissions are, of course, the responsibility of the author alone.

The author and publishers would like to thank the following organisations for permission to reproduce material in this book:

People Management (page 23), Ufi (page 32), The Open University (page 32), The National Extension College (page 32), *The Observer* (page 56), Berrier Associates (page 72–3), The Learning and Skills Council (page 80)

Edexcel examination questions are reproduced by permission of London Qualifications Ltd/Edexcel.

Photo credits: Photodisc 66 (NT), page 29; Photodisc 69 (NT), page 31.

Every effort has been made to contact copyright holders, and we apologise if any have been overlooked.

Training, Developing and Motivating People

Why businesses train staff

And how is education supposed to make me feel smarter? Besides, every time I learn something new, it pushes some old stuff out of my brain. Remember when I took that home winemaking course, and I forgot how to drive?

Homer Simpson

Introduction

Training is the passing on of skills and knowledge in order that individuals can carry out their present or future job roles effectively. Effective training that brings about the desired result should in some way benefit customers and, as a result, the firm and the individuals being trained. A main theme of this book is that training activity should be linked to the objectives of the business. Training plays an important role in achieving business objectives in a cost effective way.

Having established its objectives the business will need to make sure it has the skills it needs to meet these objectives. This will be the responsibility of the training and development function of the organisation. A skills and training audit will establish what skills the business already has and what training has taken place. This information will be the basis of a *training plan* that will identify the training needed in order to develop or update the necessary skills and knowledge to aid progress towards the business objectives and how this training will be carried out and resourced. Once training has taken place its effects should be evaluated and adjustments made to training plans as the skills and training audit information is updated.

> **Key terms**
>
> **Objectives** – targets the business will set itself.
> **Cost effective** – provides results that are value for money.

 Training and development, pages 10–13

> **Key terms**
>
> **Training and skills audit** – systematic check on skills levels and training taking place in the business.

Want to know more?

For up to date information about training and personnel matters, try this site: http://www.peoplemanagement.co.uk/

1

Reasons for training

Firms provide training to their employees for many reasons, which include the following.

Changes to consumer needs or wants

Successful businesses respond to the needs of their customers. For example, restaurants have responded to increased demand for vegetarian food by training chefs in the preparation of such meals. Suitably trained employees can respond appropriately to changes in consumer needs.

Technology

The application of new technology to the processes and techniques of business means training and updating are required. Cars have become more reliant on computer technology in the last few years so now, for example, mechanics have had to become as familiar with changing computer programmes as they are with changing oil. Businesses that adapt to new technology can gain an advantage over their competitors in terms of price, responsiveness to customer needs or cost saving.

 **CTIVITY**

Using a library or this link (http://bized.ac.uk/listserv/companies/comlist.htm) find the address of two companies and obtain copies of their annual report.
1 Establish what you think their objectives are.
2 Note how often they refer to training or staff development.

Trading conditions

As demand for a firm's products changes or new competitors appear, effective training can help the firm cope with changed trading conditions. Fifty years ago workers in most British shipyards would be trained only in one trade or narrow range of skills. Nowadays shipyard employees are more likely to have a wider range of skills. These changes have arisen as a response to increased competition from shipbuilders in countries such as Germany and Korea.

Legal

Many legal safeguards exist to protect employees and customers, and businesses need to comply with the law. The Health and Safety at Work Act (1974), for example, requires that employees receive, and co-operate with, necessary training to ensure that they work safely. Drivers of Heavy Goods Vehicles have to have the necessary training and licence, as do drivers of buses or other Public Service Vehicles before being allowed to work.

CASE STUDY

BASF training programme saves £4m

One of the world's leading chemical companies, BASF plc, recognised the benefits of training through improved business performance.

At its Seal Sands site near Middlesbrough, the implementation of a major training programme included classroom tutoring, safety training, and written assessments.

The benefits were numerous and included: the development of 150 employees towards multi-skilled self-directed teams, secured savings of £4m for 2001 due to improved performance; increased staff morale; and an improved on-site culture that attracted investment and secured the company's future in the region.

Also, other companies now use BASF plc as a good practice benchmark for adopting new training processes.

Source: Department of Trade and Industry
http://www.dti.gov.uk/training_development/case_studies.htm

Benefits of training to individuals and the business

The benefits of training to business or the individual concerned include the following.

Flexible workforce

Suitable training can increase the type of operations and services a firm can provide. This means that as consumer requirements or market conditions change the firm can more flexibly and easily respond. Early car manufacturing techniques of mass production meant that employees were restricted to a narrow range of tasks. Staff absence or changes in workload could lead to bottlenecks or slowing down of production. Manufacturers such as Volvo and Nissan have used major training programmes to help employees to become more flexible and so speed up the production process while producing cars to a higher standard.

New roles

Suitably trained staff are often better prepared for promotion or new responsibilities that can enhance their career. In many circumstances promoting staff within the firm can be more effective for the business. It avoids advertising and other costs associated with recruitment while making appointments more swiftly by internal redeployment of staff, as opposed to waiting for new employees to serve their notice before joining the organisation. This approach can improve staff loyalty to the business.

Key terms

Redeployment – Moving people to different jobs or sites within the business.
Productivity – The measure of what has been produced in relation to the resources used in production.

Improved skills

Training can improve the existing skills of staff, which will help the business while securing the employees' position with the firm as they prove their worth to the business.

Improved job performance, satisfaction and motivation

Normally employees whose job performance improves are likely to find their roles more satisfying and as a result they are better motivated. This is not only better for them in terms of individual self-belief but also better for the business.

Increased business productivity

By training employees to be better at their work and holding costs to the same levels, business productivity should improve. This results in greater profitability for the firm and, hopefully, increased job security for the individuals concerned.

New work practices

If changes in work practices designed to help business productivity and profitability are to be effectively carried out then employees will need training to help them do this.

Reduction in number of accidents and injuries

In 2001/02, 249 people were killed at work, indicating the pressing need for training to reduce risks. In manufacturing and construction in particular, training can help reduce the number of accidents and injuries. This is not only beneficial to the individuals concerned but ensures continuity of production for the business. Office workers and supervisors need also to be aware of safe working practices.

UK and European legislation

Various legal requirements affect all areas of business activities. The process of recruitment and promotion of staff, for example, requires compliance with Equal Opportunities legislation. This means that not only must staff in the personnel section of the business be aware of their legal responsibilities but supervisors and managers dealing with staff on a day-to-day basis need to ensure equality of treatment. Marketing managers are amongst those who need to be aware of the implications of the Data Protection legislation when dealing with information about customers, for example in targeting direct mail to potential customers.

⊙ASE STUDY

The Workplace Employee Relations Survey (WERS) 1998, which is the largest survey of its kind in the world, also provides compelling evidence that high performance people management practices are associated with better economic performance, better workplace well-being and a better climate of industrial relations.

The following people management policies were found to be particularly important: off-the-job training, regular performance appraisals, team working, no compulsory redundancies, problem-solving groups and family friendly working arrangements.

Businesses who employed a majority of these practices and recognised a trade union displayed above-average financial performance and experienced fewer dismissals and voluntary resignations than other businesses.

Source: Department of Trade and Industry
http://www.dti.gov.uk/greatplacetowork/evidence.htm

Reviewing training activity

Like other business processes, it is important that training activity is kept under regular review. This review should check that training activity is:

- **Meeting its objectives**. The review should establish that the planned numbers of trainees have achieved the necessary skills and knowledge and that the training has had a positive effect on business activity, e.g. reduced wastage, reduced accidents, increased output, more staff suitable for internal promotion, reduced numbers of staff leaving.
- **Linked to changing business needs**. Training should have ensured that as business processes change, employees have the necessary skills to maintain output. The introduction of new machinery, for example, should be accompanied by training ahead of, or just after, its installation.
- **Cost effective**. Efforts are needed to measure the financial benefits of training on profits in relation to the cost of training. This is not easy or straightforward. Costs include not just money paid to external trainers, for example, but work lost during training time when employees were not involved in their main jobs. Benefits or improvements following training may not be easily measurable or immediately obvious and could be due to other factors. Despite these problems it is important that some basic measures of cost and benefit are agreed and applied to the training process.

Besides taking into account the measurable benefits of training described above, any evaluation should bear in mind intangible benefits that can arise from effective training such as improved staff morale and an increased confidence in management who are seen to be investing in the business and their employees' career development.

A CTIVITY

Describe your experience of using a shop, restaurant, club or sports centre recently and identify ways in which you think the performance of the staff could have been better. How could training have helped overcome some of these problems?

Constraints on training activity

A firm's ability to provide and organise training is limited by its own internal situation, internal constraints, and by factors outside the firm, external constraints.

Internal constraints

Internal constraints include:
- financial resources
- physical resources
- staff skills.

Financial resources

In the case of financial resources, loss-making organisations, for example, will spend less on training than more profitable organisations. The loss-making firm will tend to spend money and resources on activities that it feels will have an immediate impact on improving its financial position.

Physical resources

Firms that wish to undertake training may be limited by the physical resources they have. In terms of physical resources, growing firms, for example, may have to use all their available space for the productive processes and the necessary administration. This may mean that there is no space to provide a training room. Some firms may lack sufficient physical resources to provide computers for staff undertaking training where computer applications can be used to support the training.

Staff skills

As far as staff skills are concerned, firms that are willing to provide training may lack the staff with the necessary skill to provide it to their employees. Financial constraints may combine so that they are not able to afford to pay a new employee to take on a training role. Even if they have staff with the necessary skills it is important that the firm ensures that the staff who are to be trained have the skills necessary to benefit from it and apply it in a business situation. For example, providing an advanced computer course for employees who had never used a computer before would be of little benefit to such employees or the firm as they will lack the necessary skill to understand the ideas and skills being taught.

External constraints

External constraints on training include:
- the economic situation
- legislation
- competition
- the jobs market.

Economic situation

The economic situation a business operates in will impact on its ability to provide training. High interest rates or high rates of taxation on business, for example, will increase business costs and reduce the amount of money available for training.

Legislation

The legal framework, legislation, affects a business. Individuals who wish to work as doctors or dentists, for example, have to have successfully completed training at recognised universities. Similar requirements apply in manual jobs such as gas plumbing, which can only be undertaken by CORGI (Council for Registered Gas Installers) registered operatives. The legal framework also regulates the age at which individuals can be employed and trained to drive HGV (Heavy Goods Vehicles) and PCV (Passenger Carrying Vehicles). For example, it is illegal for a driver under the age of 21 to drive a vehicle weighing more than 3,500 Kg and age restrictions apply to bus drivers.

Competition

In a competitive business situation a common response is for firms to try to reduce their costs, in order to reduce prices. This can lead to reduced spending on training. Some firms may, however, try to improve the levels of service they provide to customers and this will mean increased levels of training activity. In some of its new store openings, for example, Sainsbury's has introduced the role of Ambassador in some branches. An Ambassador will deal with customers, help them with their shopping and advise on products, and may pack the shopping for them. This role requires training in product awareness and how to deal with customers. The new role is much more skilled than the traditional supermarket bag packer.

Jobs market

The jobs market will impact on the level and type of training activity. High levels of unemployment indicate a surplus of labour in most sectors of the economy and firms may choose to recruit new staff rather than train existing employees. Low unemployment may result in shortages of staff that cause a firm to train its employees in the new skills and knowledge needed. Sometimes these trained employees may be lured to other employers, or poached, by offers of better pay and conditions. This may lead to firms reducing training and resorting to poaching to meet skills needs. This approach will create long-term problems for the economy or business sector as skills supply will never meet skills needs. The resulting shortfall will stop firms producing at the necessary levels and cause purchasers to turn towards imported goods and services if these are available.

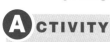

CTIVITY

Look through the last week's newspapers or news websites. From the point of view of a business of your choice how would you summarise the situation in relation to

1 the economic situation
2 legislation
3 competition
4 the jobs market?

Want to know more?

The following Department of Trade and Industry website provides examples of how training can have an impact on business success: http://www.dti.gov.uk/greatplacetowork/evidence.htm

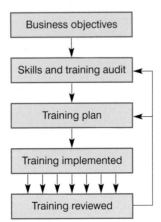

Figure 1 The role of training in achieving business objectives

The human resources training and development function

The first section of this book describes in detail why businesses train employees and why they need a training and development function. This section looks at the work of the training and development function in more detail.

Personnel systems

In order to operate efficiently a business must make good use of its labour force and strike the right balance of skilled, semi-skilled and unskilled labour. The successful firm needs to be able to select the right people for the jobs it has and ensure that its employees – the people who work for the firm – work well and are content. The business may have a centralised personnel system where a particular part of the firm deals with personnel matters. The part of the business that deals with matters relating to the workforce is the Personnel Department. In some organisations it may be called a different name such as Human Resources Department, Manpower Section or Staffing Department. Some firms have a decentralised personnel system where sections of the firm deal with their own personnel matters. Decentralised systems tend to duplicate effort, be inefficient and lack specialist personnel staff and techniques. Whatever name or system is used, each organisation needs to devote some of its efforts to looking after its staffing or personnel needs. Training and development is an important part of that process.

Training and development function

The training and development function, or work, is part of the human resource management function that promotes and supports continuous learning in the workforce. Any business, regardless of size, will have a human resource function that has, as part of its operations, a training and development function. Sole owners may do this work themselves, whereas a large company may have several staff engaged in this work.

CTIVITY

List the possible disadvantages of a centralised training and development function in a large organisation.

CASE STUDY

Efficient chips

'Two cod and chips, a scampi – deep fried, mind – some onion rings and some mushy peas, please … if you're not too grand for that now, Charlie.' There's been some right joshing since the town chippy won that posh Millennium Training Award.

But it's nice to know your chips are being wrapped by someone who's got an NVQ, or who's training for one.

Mind you, it was a bit of a blow when Charlie and Joyce Willoughby shut up shop for the day so the entire staff could travel down to the Greenwich Dome for the presentation. 'We're, well, over the moon,' Joyce says. 'Fancy a little fish and chip shop in Northumberland winning the Millennium award. It's amazing!'

And while you're waiting, take a dekko at the certificates on Charlie's walls – runner-up Daily Mail Small Business Award 1995, Alnwick District Council Innovation Award 1996, Investors in People 1996, Seafish Quality Award 1997, 98 and 99. Pride of Northumbria Award 1998 …

The couple's plans for the ultimate chippy started back in 1986, when they decided on a career change. He was a taxi-driver; she taught special needs. Charlie set to, creating the perfect recipe for cod and chips – sea-fresh fish, lightly fried in a beef dripping batter – and Joyce laid the foundations for a training culture.

'It was just simple things,' she says. 'Like telling staff the questions to ask when you're taking an order over the phone: what size of fish, any side orders?

Key terms

Training and development function
– Those activities concerned with
training and development carried out
by the business.
NVQ – National Vocational
Qualification, a nationally recognised
qualification recognising job related
skills from basic to higher levels.

 NVQ, page 82

'We wrote things down so that everyone could do them the same way.'

The checklist grew into a fully fledged training manual. It was a winning combination.

With her level 5 management NVQ, no less, Joyce is now an assessor for the Hospitality Training Foundation. She personally takes new staff through to a level 2 in food preparation and cooking, or on to the supervisory level 3.

Training has had an enormous impact on staff morale! And the award has shown what can be achieved by even the smallest business. In a traditionally low paid, seasonal sector, training motivates staff by recognising their achievements and giving them confidence to move on to better paid work.

Elsie Stewart was 51 when she got her certificate in food hygiene at Charlie's – her first paper qualification. Now she's mid-level 2, and attending outreach classes in IT by Northumberland College, Ashington, and she's a shift manager. Morag, the counter assistant, has all but lost her stammer and loves the quick banter of a busy chip shop counter.

'They've all gained in confidence,' Joyce says. 'They see training as part of their job – they are contributing to a growing business.'

Charlie and Joyce now have bigger fish to fry, and are branching out into creating and evaluating training materials and offering bespoke training for small businesses. Eat your heart out, Harry Ramsden!

The Guardian, 7 March 2000

Employee training and development

Successful businesses develop their goods and services so that customers' demands are anticipated and satisfied. To be able to develop goods and services it is important that a firm's employees are kept up to date with changes and developments that affect their jobs and careers. This not only benefits the firm but also the employees' future job prospects. Staff training and development starts when an employee joins the organisation and undergoes induction training and continues right up to when the employee leaves the firm.

Training methods are covered in more detail in the next section but we should note at this point that they range from the informal – short conversations, copying how others work – to more formal highly structured methods such as attending classes at a college, university or firm's training centre for a period of weeks, months or years in order to receive a formal qualification such as a degree, National Certificate or NVQ.

 Training methods, page 24

Key term

Informal training – where
employees learn from each other in
an unstructured, unplanned
spontaneous manner.

Effective training and development involves:
- identifying human resource development needs
- skills auditing
- planning, designing and delivery of training
- evaluation of training.

Identifying human resource development needs

This should be done in line with the business objectives of the organisation. Clear business objectives will indicate the job roles that will be needed to achieve these objectives.

Each job role will require employees to have particular skills, knowledge and attitudes. Before a definite conclusion can be reached about the organisation's skills needs consideration should be given to the current types and levels of skills in the organisation. A skills audit can provide this information (see below).

 Business objectives, page 1

 **ACTIVITY**

With reference to older or retired employees, textbooks or newspapers make a list of skills needed to work as an office administrator now and those needed to do the same job 20 years ago. What are the differences and similarities?

Skills auditing

This is done in order to identify organisational and individual planning needs. Skills auditing can be done through an analysis of up-to-date appraisal and training records, where they exist. These records should indicate which employees have undertaken different types of training and how recent it was. The application and interview records of new employees should also yield information about the skills of the new appointees. Where these records are not in place or are not sufficiently detailed a skills survey could be undertaken. This could be in the form of a questionnaire or interview where employees are asked about training activities they have undertaken and other skills they may have developed as part of their outside activities. For example, manual workers who undertake voluntary youth work could be expected to have a good degree of interpersonal and organisational skill that their manual job does not require or allow them to demonstrate.

 Appraisal and training records, page 68

Key term
....
Skills gap – the difference between the skills the firm currently has and the skills it expects to need in the future.

 **CASE STUDY**

Why PAs are up for IT

Before you stifle a yawn at the prospect of a career switch to IT, consider this. There's a dearth of talent and an expected glut of (better-paid) jobs. You might be paid to retrain. Your skills – business knowledge, communication, organisation, problem-solving, etc – mean you're more than halfway there already. Don't think nerdy software and backroom techies, think of a pacy, vibrant industry.

11

'The beauty of PAs and secretaries is that they already know the business inside out – companies fall down when they hire technical people who have no skills outside their area,' says Colin Steed, chief executive of the Institute of IT Training.

'In my experience, PAs are wonderful organisers,' agrees Maxine Mayer, project manager at the e-skills National Training Organisation. 'They also have excellent customer services skills – these are totally transferable.'

Interested? You should consider your options. But where among the vast array of IT careers should you focus, and how can you get there? There are jobs for every aptitude from the more technically minded, such as website and multimedia design, IT maintenance and administration, to the softer skilled jobs, such as training and support. 'IT services – engineering and the like – have a horrible image,' says Mayer. 'Some see it as oily, greasy, heavy work – it's none of those things, and women can do it.'

'Beware of rushing blindly into expensive training without exploring cheaper options,' warns Roisin Woolnough of Computer Weekly. IT skills can date quickly and you can often glean more from your own – and colleagues' – computers. 'Everyone is talking about a skills shortage, but training is no good without experience,' she cautions. 'Experience counts more than degrees or qualifications. Why not speak to your employers, explain that you're interested, and get training at the expense of the company.'

Which is what Louise Jeffrey, former PA to the head of Random House, did when she felt she'd outgrown her administrational duties. At a time when the publishers were developing the website, she stepped in with enthusiasm and an insider's knowledge of the company. She's now web administrator for Random House and Transworld – working alongside a webmaster to produce a site that promotes books and attracts new users.

Former receptionist Ingrid Jonkman has chosen a different route into IT – and one open to most PAs with good communications skills. She's working alongside colleagues with IT degrees – on a diagnostic help-desk service offered by the IT management firm Pink Elephant. 'I'd grown bored with my job, and I had to convince [Pink Elephant] that I was really determined to move.'

More important than acquiring technical skills – the majority of which Jonkman has learnt on the job or through computer-based training – was to prove she has the customer skills required to handle irate calls and provide over-the-phone advice. 'I'm never bored now, and there are so many different directions and managerial openings in this area.'

The Guardian, 16 July 2001 http://www.guardian.co.uk/

Want to know more?

For information about skills shortages and employer surveys go to:
http://skillsbase.dfes.gov.uk/default.asp

Planning, designing and delivery of training

Once the information from a skills audit has been linked to the
projected skills needs the business can make a judgement about the
'skills gap' it has to bridge. In other words the firm will be aware of what
skills it has in its present position and what it needs to get to its
objectives. It then needs to plan how it will move forward to bridge the
gap in order to achieve its objectives. This may involve appointing staff
from outside with the necessary skills as well as planning, designing and
delivering suitable training to existing employees.

Figure 2 *Bridging the skills gap
requires good judgement*

Evaluation of training

Judgements about training activity are important to identify the costs
and benefits to the organisation and the individuals involved. The first
section describes some of the ways training can be reviewed and
evaluated.

 Reviewing training
activity, page 5 and
pages 21–23

ACTIVITY

A trainer costs £25 per hour. Overtime for three staff to do the work of three production assembly line workers attending a six-hour training course costs £10.00 per hour each. What is the cost of this training event? What other costs need to be considered when establishing the true cost of a training programme? How would you judge if this was value for money?

Training and development policy

Larger organisations will find it useful to have a training and development policy so that staff at all levels are aware of the requirements of the organisation and their own rights and responsibilities. Quantified statements of the organisation's commitment to training and development in the policy give an exact indication of the firm's commitment and help the financial planning of training and development activity. The policy might indicate, for example, the number of days annually each employee can have for training and development. It could identify an amount of money per person the firm will spend on provision of training and development each year. The firm's commitment might alternatively be described as a percentage of its wages bill annually that the business will spend on training and development.

The training and development policy will guide the work and planning of the training and development function and have a range of content that, in addition to the items mentioned above, would normally include statements about things such as:

- the benefits to the organisation of having a training and development policy
- the benefits of training and development to staff and the organisation
- responsibilities of various staff members for training and development
- personal development as an individual responsibility within the organisation
- the firm's commitment to acknowledge and reward improved performance
- the firm's intention to use improved skills where it can
- arrangements for individual career planning
- a description of what the business will provide for training and development
- a list of training and development methods used in the organisation
- facilities for learning during work time
- rules relating to paid or unpaid leave for training and development purposes.

The annual implementation of the policy will be guided by a training plan that is the responsibility of the training and development function.

Planning, resourcing and evaluating training

If you go through a lot of hammers each month, I don't think it
necessarily means you're a hard worker. It may just mean that you
have a lot to learn about proper hammer maintenance.

Jack Handy

In order for training to benefit the business and the individual it must be
carefully planned to meet specific needs. In order for the planned
training to be effective it will need to be adequately resourced in terms
of staffing and other support needed to make the training intervention
effective. Once the training has been completed those involved should
evaluate how well it met the initial objectives and what factors helped or
limited the effectiveness of the training. It is important that the training
activity has a positive impact on the running and operation of the
business. These stages are outlined below.

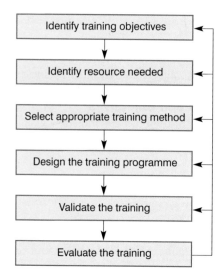

Figure 3 *The stages involved in
planning training*

Planning training programmes

The training activity of the business should support the achievement of
its overall business objectives. Even in small firms the range of training
needs will be broad. Training needs may range from basic first aid or how
to lift heavy objects safely to advanced computer programming or high
level accountancy. The training activity a firm undertakes will be made
up of a series of training programmes aimed at meeting specific training
needs. Although the programmes may be very different, the planning
involved will go through basically the same stages.

Skills audit, page 11

Identify training objectives

The objectives of any training activity will be based on the perceived needs of the business and the individuals within it. Information about training needs can be gained from several sources. These sources contribute to what we describe as a skills audit. These sources are described below.

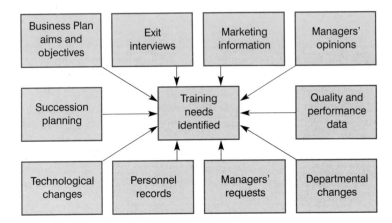

Figure 4 Sources of information about training needs

Intelligent use of these sources in combination will greatly assist the development of training objectives that meet business needs.

Business plan aims and objectives
These set the direction of the business and show what its priorities are in future.

Exit interviews
Interviewing employees who are leaving the firm can be a way of finding out areas they think can be improved.

Marketing information
Changes in customer requirements or the behaviour of competitors can indicate skills or knowledge that the business should develop.

Managers' opinions
Managers have a range of experience, knowledge and skills that should be used in planning training activity.

Quality and performance data
Information about things like wastage rates, sales levels, performance against targets and customer satisfaction surveys can show where previous training has been effective or where in the business there is a need for further training activity.

Departmental changes

Departmental reorganisations may result in changed responsibilities that should be supported through training to develop suitable knowledge and skills.

Managers' requests

Departmental or other managers may make requests for particular training for them or their staff in order to help them make their contribution to the business.

Personnel records

Information about individual employees' previous qualifications, interests, performance or experience should be used to inform the training that is provided to them.

Technological changes

New computers and other modern equipment bring with them associated training needs for most individuals.

Succession planning

Knowing that an employee with important skills is about to leave the business, perhaps for a new job or retirement, should cause a response that could involve training another individual in the firm to carry out the duties of the person who is due to leave.

Objectives of training

At the outset it is essential that the people planning the training are clear about what they want to achieve as a result of the training. The more specific these objectives are the better.

A common approach is to express the objectives in terms of what the trainees will be able to do at the end of the training as a result of their participation. For example, 'At the end of the course trainees will be able to safely operate the deep fat fryer used in the hotel kitchens' is quite specific about what will be achieved. Being clear about the objectives in advance is important for several reasons. In particular it guides training organisers in what needs to be done by them to achieve the objectives and also lets training participants know in advance what the outcomes will be so that they can decide whether participation is worthwhile. The objective should be clear about how the training will affect the participants' behaviour in their job.

> **Key terms**
>
> **Objective** – thing that a person, business, training course or other individual or groups set out to achieve.

ACTIVITY

In relation to a business you use, work for or are familiar with, write down the aims for some training you think would be of benefit to the staff or customers.

Identify resources needed

The resources needed to carry out training should be established at the
planning stage. Trainers will need to consider the following.

Finance

The cost of the training should consider not only the obvious things like
room hire and presenters' fees but also the cost of lost production or the
employment of replacement staff to carry out the duties of those
undergoing training. At the same time finance discussions should
consider sources of external funding. The European Union provides
funding for activities in defined categories through the European Social
Fund (ESF). The categories change over time but usually are aimed at
helping individuals find work or develop skills in areas of skill shortage.
Learning and Skills Councils (LSCs) fund training through colleges and
other providers but may make training grants available in areas of
specific need. Modern Apprenticeships, for example, are LSC funded.

Individuals can finance their own full- or part-time training through
initiatives such as the Career Development loan which is provided at
low interest through banks to support individuals' learning.

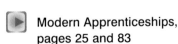

Modern Apprenticeships,
pages 25 and 83

Personnel

Using the various sources of information the trainer will need to decide
which members of staff would benefit from the proposed training activity.
This can involve negotiation with the individuals and/or their manager
to get their commitment to take part in the activity.

Consideration should be given to who will be involved in providing
the training. Do you use experienced and skilled people from inside the
business or do you use personnel from outside organisations? The choice
of personnel may have a financial impact.

Time

Decisions about how much time to allocate to the training activity are
important, as is the decision about the timing of the event; for example,
at what point in the working week it should take place. Various days and
times may have to be discarded as options if the event is likely to disrupt
critical business activity that takes place on that day. For example, taking
the wages department staff to a training event on the day that final
wages calculations would normally be completed could be considered
disruptive, particularly if it meant that staff wages were delayed.

Location

Some training, particularly that involving specialist equipment, may be
held in the place of work. Other activities may require facilities available
elsewhere. Some events are better held away form the workplace if the
trainer wants to minimise interruptions or distractions from the
workplace.

Equipment

Care should be given to identify equipment that might be used to improve presentations or involve the trainees. Overhead projectors and flip charts are common and greater use is now being made of digital projectors. Any tools or other resources that participants may need should be identified in advance and decisions about who will provide resources communicated to participants and trainers well in advance of the event.

Materials

The issues with materials are similar to those with equipment. Trainers should indicate, well in advance, what materials participants should provide for themselves. Where trainers are providing materials such as notes or booklets these should be of a high quality. Written materials should take account of the previous education of the participants. For example, the language used in handouts to members of an MBA course would be different from the language used in handouts to employees undergoing training in the correct use of street cleaning equipment.

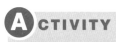**CTIVITY**

Review classes or training sessions you have attended and, of the methods that were used to teach you, list which ones you enjoyed most and which ones you enjoyed least. Compare your list with that of someone else in the group. Which training methods were the most and least popular?

Select appropriate training methods

Training is usually undertaken either 'on the job' – in other words in the actual place of work as part of the work process, or 'off the job' – away from the work process. The next section deals with individual training methods in more detail.

 On the job and off the job training, pages 20–21

Design the training programme

The training programme should have clear **objectives**, related to a business need and communicated and understood by everyone involved in the training activity. A **budget** for the training should be established to cover costs of trainers, venues, materials, equipment, travel, accommodation if necessary and other appropriate associated costs. The **administrative arrangements** to support the programme should be clear. Responsibilities for booking required staff and facilities and producing course resources should be established and action taken well in advance of the programme. The identification of **participants** is critical. They may nominate themselves, be nominated by their manager or come to the programme as a result of a training need identified during appraisal or some other performance management activity. Decisions about training methods should have particular regard to the participants and the aims of the training. The methods chosen should be those that are most likely to meet the aims for the participants while staying within the identified budget.

Validate the training

Validation means that the training is recognised in some way, and validated training is more likely to be recognised and understood by potential employers. The simplest form of validation is for the training provider to issue a certificate indicating that the person named on the certificate has attended the course and giving a brief outline of what the training covered. Training can be validated by external organisations. For example, the St John's Ambulance Brigade validates first aid training. Provided the training covers what the Brigade deems necessary and the learner is able to prove they are competent a certificate will be issued. Other organisations validate training, often requiring some combination of course work, portfolio development, externally set test or practical exercise. AVCEs offered by OCR, AQA or Edexcel are examples of validated learning, as are qualifications offered by the AAT (Association of Accounting Technicians). Before organisations can offer validated training they have to prove to the validating body that they have the necessary skills, resources and quality systems to deliver their awards reliably.

Want to know more?

Edexcel and OCR are awarding bodies that can help validate learning. Their websites offer further details: www.edexcel.org.uk/ and www.ocr.org.uk/

 On the job training methods, pages 20–29

 Off the job training methods, pages 30–32

Evaluate the training

On the job and off the job training have their own particular related advantages and disadvantages. Some of the advantages and disadvantages of particular methods of training are mentioned in the next section. These should also be considered when training is being evaluated. It is possible, however, to make some general observations about the merits of on and off the job training.

On the job training

On the job training allows individuals to develop and practise work-related skills, e.g. selling, administration, manual. Some productive output is achieved at the same time as the person is learning and developing skills and knowledge. Linkages between theory and practice are more immediate and learners can see the work-related relevance of what they are learning. Learning is linked to the day-to-day work and performance management system.

The quality of guidance and support for learners is critical to how effective on the job learning is likely to be. Unless managers and supervisors are committed to this approach and have the necessary skills to support this form of learning the result may be that bad habits are re-enforced and learners become demotivated. The distractions of the workplace may deflect the attention of the learner to other tasks and duties, rather than the skills and knowledge that they are supposed to acquire. Identifying the successful outcomes that are required may help to focus learners and their managers/supervisors on the acquisition of the necessary skills and knowledge.

Off the job training

Off the job training allows the learner to focus on acquiring the skills and knowledge necessary for their job. Off the job training commonly allows learners access to high quality instruction and support which can increase motivation and help them identify with the aims of the business. Off the job training can be said to be particularly useful in developing specialised skills and knowledge and broadening participants' horizons by meeting people from other workplaces. This approach avoids the distractions and demands of the workplace. This may also be a disadvantage as learners have to be able to transfer their learning from the training situation to 'real life', and this may be difficult unless the training has helped them prepare for this.

Evaluating training activities

Specific training activities should be evaluated against the original aims and objectives to see how far these have been achieved. Effective evaluation should consider four aspects of the training activity as discussed below.

Participant reaction

Responses from those who took part in the training activity can provide insight into how effective the training was. Reactions can be sought in relation to how the training related to the aims and objectives as well as how the training related to the learners' work situation. End of course questionnaires or discussion sessions are common ways of getting participant reactions. As well as informing evaluations about the training content trainers can learn a lot from participant reactions about the best ways to organise the learning activities.

Participant learning

Learning can be evaluated to measure how far the skills, knowledge or attitudes of the learners have changed as a result of participating in the training activity. Pre- and post-training tests of participants' skills, attitudes and knowledge can help the trainer evaluate how much has been learned as a result of the training activity. Written or computer tests can be used to do this, as can observation and questioning. Validated training will commonly involve some degree of written assessment of learning.

Participant behaviour

Evaluation of the participants' behaviour in the workplace will indicate the extent to which the skills, knowledge or attitudes that were developed in the training activity have been transferred to the place of work. Appraisal and performance management activity will give some indication of the impact of the training on the learners' behaviour. For behavioural evaluation to be effective it should be based on an accurate understanding of the participants' pre-training performance and behaviour.

Business results

The impact of training on the business activities it sets out to support is an important measure in understanding whether the cost of training can be justified. The link is a far from easy one to prove. Quantifiable changes in things like sales, customer satisfaction surveys, wastage rates, productivity levels and accidents are useful sources of evidence in evaluating the impact of training. This provides a cost benefit analysis

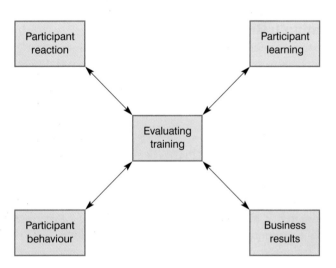

Figure 5 Effective evaluation is as
important as training is to help
business development

where the benefits of the training are quantified against the costs and a judgement taken about the effectiveness of the training intervention.

Evaluation of training should give good information with the lowest levels of cost and inconvenience in gathering the information.

CASE STUDY

Happy Sheets are not enough

The evaluation of training and development is still not being taken seriously enough, HRD delegates were told. Angela Hatton, senior partner at training and marketing consultancy Tactics, said that research drawn from the CIPD's Training and Development 2003 survey showed many organisations were still not formally evaluating training beyond producing 'happy sheets' at the end of events.

Trainers poured time and effort into producing and analysing these sheets, when they tended to show mostly what was wrong with the catering, it was heard.

'The reality is too few people are taking evaluation of training and development seriously,' Hatton told delegates.

Trainers should be 'driving both the efficiency and effectiveness of their activities' if they wanted to be successful. The CIPD research did suggest that an increasing number of organisations are setting training objectives in terms of business benefits. But Hatton said this needed to be followed up by changes in their evaluation strategies.

Drawing on her marketing expertise, Hatton likened current training evaluation processes to having to justify the cost of individual adverts within a planned marketing campaign. But trainers needed to focus on the whole picture.

'In terms of business benefit, value is only added when learning is applied to the business,' said Hatton. 'Training is only one ingredient in this process.'

Line managers, other stakeholders and the rewards system were equally important to improving performance, she said. However, training and development departments frequently didn't see it as their job to align these to ensure business benefits were delivered.

Hatton said that any trainers who were evaluating their training and not making changes as a result needed to question their evaluation processes.

'It's not how much time we spend on evaluation. It's the use we make of the intelligence that shows we have the right approaches,' she concluded.

*Source: Originally published in People Management (17 April 2003)
and reproduced with permission*

| Training methods

You cannot teach a man anything; you can only help him find it within himself.

Galileo Galilei

The last section looked at the broad categories of on and off the job training. This section looks at some of the individual methods that come within each category and considers them from the point of view of employer and learner.

On the job training methods

These include the following.

Job shadowing

The job shadowing approach involves the learner accompanying the jobholder throughout their normal working activity and observing the processes involved. Employees who are being prepared for promotion or change of role can benefit from job shadowing if it is well planned. This approach allows the learner to see at first hand what is involved in the job. It is important at the outset that the learner and the person being shadowed have an understanding of what the outcomes will be in terms of learning and that the learner has an opportunity to ask questions to gain insight into what they are observing. It can be argued that the presence of the observer changes the working environment of the jobholder and makes the experience less realistic as a result. The observer involved in the shadowing is usually unable to make a significant contribution to the work being done while being unable to complete their own work, so making this approach less effective in terms of immediate contribution to business activity. Whilst this may be a disadvantage for the employer, this form of training is cheap and convenient for employer and employee alike.

Coaching

This is one-to-one support that aims to develop skills and attitudes. Good coaching gives the learner feedback on their performance while at the same time giving them increased responsibility for aspects of the job. Coaching takes place on the job, and so makes use of real work situations. This approach uses discussion and reflection to guide and advise the learner about appropriate responses, rather than giving specific instructions about what to do and when to do it. Coaching is commonly employed in situations where the role involves leading others or planning work and in situations where there are a number of possible responses to the situations the employee has to deal with. From the employer's point of view the benefits of coaching are not always readily observable, although it is a form of training that is cheap and causes little disruption to business activity. Employees find it convenient and tailored to their own personal circumstances while avoiding loss of earnings, such as productivity bonus, through being sent away to an off the job programme.

Job rotation

Job rotation involves individuals changing jobs periodically. This approach exposes the learner to a variety of roles and responsibilities. At its best it is a planned set of experiences. These can develop specifically planned skills and knowledge related to each job situation in which employees find themselves, at the same time as they make a contribution to the work of the business. Involving the learner in setting the objectives for the rotation in terms of what they might learn and then reviewing these periodically is important. The end result is an employee with an enhanced set of skills and a broader practical understanding of a range of business activities. At its worst job rotation is an excursion to different parts of the business where the learner is tolerated, makes a limited contribution to the work of the business and the degree of learning is left to chance. Feelings of frustration by employee and host department can result. Job rotation allows the employee to build up a network of contacts in the business that can be useful later in their career. From an employer's point of view job rotation is a good way of developing employees' skills without the cost of a training course but it can lead to lost productivity or waste as the learner comes to terms with the new job. The employee has the benefit of developing a range of skills that improves the career progression opportunities.

Apprenticeships

Apprenticeships normally last between a minimum of one and three years and there are two levels: Foundation (FMA) and Advanced (AMA) at NVQ Levels 2 and 3 respectively. They each lead to:

- National Vocational Qualifications (NVQ) – providing practical skills in specific occupational areas (see below)
- Key Skills qualifications – transferable work-related skills like IT and communication, application of number, problem solving, teamwork and improving learning and performance
- Technical certificates – vocationally related qualifications that provide the underpinning knowledge of the NVQ.

Employers are responsible for various aspects of the apprenticeship scheme, with support from the LSC. Employers need to address several important issues for their Modern Apprentices:

- on the job training – inducting the apprentice into their role and providing on the job training opportunities
- salary – paying apprentices in full-time employment
- recruitment – taking an active part in the recruitment of the apprentice

> ### Key terms
>
> **National Vocational Qualifications (NVQs)** – qualifications awarded on the basis of what the learner can do in relation to a particular occupation.
> **Apprenticeships** – most apprenticeships offered by business today are Modern Apprenticeships, organised and sponsored by the government's Learning and Skills Council (LSC). The scheme covers around 150 vocational areas.

> ### Key term
>
> **LSC (Learning and Skills Council)** – a government organisation whose role is to promote and help organise training and learning for those over school leaving age. There are currently 47 local Learning and Skills councils across Britain, supported by a central LSC organisation.

- time for learning – giving apprentices enough time and resources for training, which may be off the job, and assessment commitments
- review – contributing to the regular review of the apprentice's progress.

If employers are not in a position to employ the apprentice under this scheme they can opt for a work placement. Modern Apprentices who are on work placements receive a guaranteed training allowance paid by the Learning and Skills Council.

Want to know more?

The central LSC website provides links to the activities of each of the 47 local LSCs: www.lsc.gov.uk/

CASE STUDY

A North East brewery is showing it has the bottle to succeed by encouraging its staff to improve their production skills with training provider, assa.

A total of 26 employees from the Federation Brewery's packaging department have just completed NVQ Level 2 in Performing Manufacturing Operations with the training specialist.

The brewery recently invested £5 million in two new production lines to expand the packaging part of the organisation and, as part of the implementation of new machinery, a customised training programme was needed to embed new procedures and to raise the standards of staff across the board.

After hearing about assa's Accreditation of Manufacturing Staff programme, the brewery approached the company to devise a training plan suitable to meet its requirements.

T Magazine, March 2003

Competence based training (NVQs)

Competence is not easily defined. We prefer to use the following definition: 'All the work-related personal attributes, knowledge, skills and values that a person draws upon to do their work well.' (G Roberts, *Recruitment and Selection: a competency approach*, Institute of Personnel and Development, 1997)

Any training that tries to develop measurable behaviour that can be observed and assessed is competence based training. In the UK the competence based approach is used in National Vocational Qualifications (NVQs). Each NVQ relates to a particular occupation. A functional analysis of the occupation linked to each NVQ has been carried out. Functional analysis breaks down jobs into their sub-tasks. This process indicates what people in particular roles have to do and the standards of performance that they would normally be expected to meet to be competent at the particular role. These statements of sub-tasks related to a job role form the basis of the qualification and individuals are assessed in the workplace to ascertain whether or not they have met these standards. NVQs are not graded in the way, for example, AVCE qualifications are. Assessment ascertains if the person is competent or not yet competent. Certificates are issued when competence is demonstrated, as with other recognised qualifications. The assessment of NVQs in the workplace can only be carried out by assessors who have vocational experience and appropriate qualifications, such as the D32/33 award. The complex language, quality control and documentation procedures associated with NVQs add to the cost of their implementation and have limited their uptake. Their relevance to the workplace seems to vary from business to business, although a number of large employers make use of them, and as they provide recognition for work-related skills thousands of individuals have gained the certification. NVQs are commonly linked to apprenticeships.

 Apprenticeships, page 25

Competence based training, in many cases, allows the learner to gain recognition for the skills they have without the inconvenience of attending further training. For both learner and employer the recording systems used in this approach can be complex and time-consuming.

Computer based training (CBT)

The use of computers to provide highly structured learning via CD, company intranet or the internet is a feature of modern learning. The better computer based training is interactive. Learners will be guided to the next set of tasks according to how they performed in earlier tasks. Material will be presented as text, graphics and video in order to maintain variety. Large firms of accountants use this approach for professional updating of staff to ensure compliance with professional standards, while in other contexts it is used to demonstrate manual lifting techniques for staff in builders' merchants. Feedback to the learner can be fast and accurate and so re-enforce positive learning and increase learner motivation. CBT is a feature of some aspects of distance learning. CBT is convenient for employees and for the employers has the advantage of not being disruptive of work activity. CBT materials can be expensive to purchase.

 Off the job training methods, page 30

CASE STUDY

The Hitchhiker's Guide to E-learning

Before starting any type of e-learning initiative, it's important to know your intended audience. Understanding your users is the most important step in the e-learning development process: If users are not satisfied with the final e-learning course, the course will not be effective, utilised or even purchased. How does one learn about users? The answer is simple: Talk with them. Conduct site visits with a representative sample of your intended user audience and learn about the users, their education needs and work environments.

Using what you have learned about users, the next step is to determine the appropriate presentation media to be used in the e-learning course. For example, you may decide that users should simply read on-screen text, or you may decide that users should listen to audio narration. You may also determine that video demonstrations or interactive workshops would be effective for your user population. Finally, a combination of presentation media may provide the most effective learning experience for your users.

Your decisions concerning the presentation media will influence the technical format of the e-learning course. The available formats include Internet delivery, CD-ROM delivery or synchronous learning (i.e. virtual classroom). At this stage, it is important to remember the limitations of your users' technical environments. Streaming video and audio, for example, will not perform well on a slower dial-up Internet connection. If users have a slow Internet connection (or no connection), you may want to consider CD-ROM deployment.

Once you have determined the format of the e-learning, it's time to develop the educational content. The development phase of your e-learning initiative will require your best project management skills. Before you begin actual development, you and your development staff should agree on the overall scope of the final course. A project plan, properly drafted and agreed to by all project participants, will help ensure that the desired end result is attained within a reasonable timeframe and budget.

It's important to revisit your users before actual development begins. You will receive a tremendous amount of feedback by simply presenting your users with drawings of proposed screen and menu layouts. The best advice here is 'always test; never assume.'

If you want your e-learning course to be eligible for continuing professional education (CPE) credit (Validation), additional usability testing will be required. CPE credit sponsorship granted through National Association of State Boards of Accountancy (NASBA) requires an independent review of your course by licensed certified public accountants.

[Note: The accreditation system referred to in the paragraph above applies to United States accreditation; the UK system is different.]

Before selling your wares, consider how you will deploy the course to users. If you deliver your content as a virtual classroom course, the users will have to connect real time to your site or to the third party site that hosts your virtual session. If you deploy your course as computer-based training, then the deployment will simply involve delivering or shipping CD-ROMs. Regardless of the deployment scenario, you should ensure that the server and infrastructure can support the expected volume of users.

The deployment method and security tie in closely with pricing and licensing options. Regardless of the pricing model used, it is important that you price your course according to the value that it provides to the client. As a benchmark, you may want to compare the price of your course to the price of a traditional lecture-based class on the same content. Reminding clients of the cost of classroom training (including ancillary costs like travel, lodging, and meals) often helps justify the price for your e-learning application.

Source: G. Alan Davis is director of education at John Daniels Associates, Inc.

Based on an article in Trainingmag.com April 2003

Figure 6 *Computer based training is convenient for people with access to a computer.*

Off the job training methods

These include the following.

In-house courses

This approach involves the business providing its own facilities and resources for training to take place away from the workplace. Larger organisations, such as the Civil Service or major banks, may have their own training centres while others will hire space elsewhere. Many businesses will have access to meeting rooms or dedicated on-site facilities where training can take place. Courses may be led by specialist trainers or those with technical skills from the business, by outside specialists or by some combination. For both employer and learner, in-house courses have the advantage of being linked to business need and providing learning linked to specific business activity. This is more likely to help production from the employer's point of view and, for the learner, has the potential to increase their earnings or career progression in the firm.

External courses

External courses can be provided by local FE colleges, universities or specialist training organisations. They have the advantage of using suitably qualified and experienced staff and good resources. The disadvantage for employer and learner is that the courses may not relate to specific business needs and be too general in their approach. Timing may be inconvenient. External courses give learners the opportunity to mix with others in a similar situation to themselves and develop different perspectives to their work.

Bought-in training

A business may 'buy-in' external trainers if it lacks the specialist skills to provide its own training and is concerned about external courses being too general. Training can be bought from a specialist training organisation, an industry organisation or by providers of specialist equipment and machinery. FE colleges and universities commonly offer training on this basis. Bought-in training providers should attempt to reflect and understand the business needs of the organisation and ensure that the training offered is relevant and provides a solution to the problems the business has identified. Bought-in training can be of a technical nature related to the firm's production activity or may relate to improving motivation, communication or some other aspects of the business process. Bought-in training can be timed to suit the business.

Placements

Businesses can develop their personnel by placing them in situations outside of their organisation. This may be done full-time for a lengthy period of time or for as little as half a day a month. Well organised placements help the learner to develop a range of skills. BAe for many years has encouraged staff to work in local schools, helping students

Figure 7 Off the job training avoids
the distraction of the workplace.

develop reading and other skills; KPMG staff are involved in a range of
community activities, such as school governorships. The Business in the
Community organisation from time to time helps local community
groups with advice and expertise on business matters. Arguments in
favour of placements are that they broaden the outlook of the learner,
help them develop an external network and enable the firm to
contribute to its community. Learning aims need to be identified in
advance of the placement and regular reviews undertaken to ensure
these are being met. Otherwise the learner can feel isolated from their
own organisation and lose sight of the original aims of the placement.

Simulations

By combining case studies and role play learners are guided through
situations that are intended to be as realistic as possible. Learners can
practise behaviour, communication and decision making in as realistic a
situation as the trainers can provide. This gives learners the opportunity
to think about their actions, with support from the trainers, in a way
that is not possible in the workplace. Army war games are one sort of
simulation but businesses can use this approach for a range of situations
such as making a sales presentation, or managing a factory production
line or other situations where learners need to handle information,
analyse it and communicate with others. This approach means that,
unlike some aspects of on the job learning, poor decisions have no
impact on business activity, which is beneficial to the employer.

Distance learning

This approach uses specially prepared material and involves the learner learning at home at a time that it is suitable for them. Distance learning is often used in combination with computer based training (CBT).

The Open University offers a range of undergraduate and postgraduate degrees, diplomas, certificates and NVQs using a system called supported open learning in which print, video, audio, computer programmes and web materials are supported by personal tuition and web conferencing with other students. learndirect, Ufi's network of e-learning services, offers a range of programmes to suit a range of skills and abilities, mainly using CBT approaches. The National Extension College (NEC) is another distance learning provider offering customised distance learning solutions for organisations and companies as well as individual home study courses and open learning resources. Independent learning is achieved through a combination of paper-based or online course materials and back-up from a specialist tutor accessible via the phone, e-mail or by post. Learners also have the option to join online community areas to interact with other students. Distance learning is not usually a cheap method of learning but it is convenient for employees who can adjust the timing of their learning to suit their personal circumstances. Distance learning reduces the time the learner is away from the workplace, to the benefit of the employer.

Figure 8 *Distance learning providers*

ACTIVITY

Name two specific training methods that you think are most likely to suit each of the following types of learners:

- 16-year-old school leaver with three GCSEs who wishes to work as a shop assistant
- 35-year-old graduate, travelling salesman often away from home who wishes to gain a higher qualification in Sales and Marketing
- 48-year-old experienced deputy manager who has been identified as a possible senior manager when the present post holder retires in six months
- a group of 17 production managers in a multinational company who need to become familiar with new factory management techniques.

Motivation at work

Mr. Scorpio says productivity is up 2%, and it's all because of my motivational techniques, like donuts and the possibility of more donuts to come.

Homer Simpson

What is motivation?

If we have a reason to do something, the desire for doughnuts for example, we have a motive. Motivation is a process that results from having a goal, some may say a need, and making efforts to achieve it. Work and learning are some of the behaviours people display in order to achieve their goals or satisfy their needs. Other, less desirable, behaviours might be robbery or fraud. Motivation is a state of mind and not something that can be seen. One way we can judge how well motivated an individual may be is by observing the efforts they make to achieve their goals.

If businesses are to achieve their goals managers need to be able to relate and link the needs and motivation of individuals to achieving the business's goals. Organisational objectives should therefore take account of individual needs and motivation. One of the key skills of managers and supervisors is to be able to identify how organisational needs might conflict with individual needs and then find ways of dealing with this so that the business continues to be effective and its individuals continue to be motivated. Workplace nurseries, for example, are one way in which some firms have resolved the conflict between employees' childcare needs and the firm's desire to have people in work regularly and on time.

Every individual is different and has different needs and motivation. Researchers have attempted to understand motivation in depth and arrived at a number of theories or ideas about what motivates people.

We consider these below and then go on to look at the practical
application of these theories to working life.

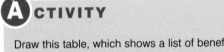

Draw this table, which shows a list of benefits offered by a number of
employers. Summarise the impact for employers and employees in the
relevant column and discuss in a group, to identify which is the most
important from employer's and employees' point of view. The first one has
been done for you.

Benefit	Impact on employee	Impact on employer
On-site subsidised nursery	Reassurance of childcare, not distracted by arrangements.	Employee can focus on work, develops employee loyalty.
Interest free season ticket loan		
Flexi-time working		
Payment of external course fees		
Bonus related to individual sales		
Bonus related to company sales		
Effective active policies to promote diversity		

Theories of motivation

As in any type of research activity there are a variety of theories about
motivation. These can be classified as broadly being of two types:

- Instrumentalist theory
- Content theory.

Instrumentalist theory

This theory was developed in the late nineteenth and early twentieth
centuries. Based on the works of F W Taylor, and his principles of
scientific management, it assumes that people will work best if rewards
and penalties are closely linked to their performance. For this theory to
work in practice, workers need to be promptly and regularly rewarded
when they do well and, similarly, punished when they do poorly. It may
appear an attractive theory but fails to take account of the practicalities
of the informal relationships in the workplace that may distort its
operation and the fact that individuals may be motivated by more than
just external factors like pay and penalties.

Needs (Content) theory

Needs theory arose from the works of Abraham Maslow in 1954. Maslow categorised human needs in a hierarchy made up of five levels, with physical needs at the base and social needs at the apex.

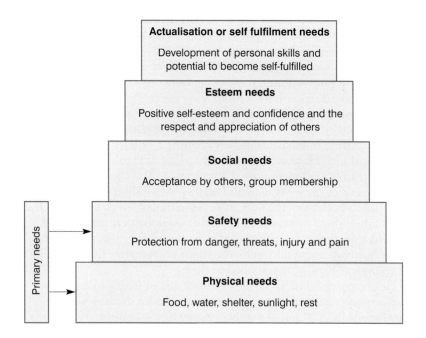

Figure 9 *Maslow's hierarchy of needs gives a simplified view of human needs*

Maslow argued that people were motivated to satisfy each level of need and then would move up to attempt to satisfy the needs that existed at the next level. Self-fulfilment would never be totally achieved but would be a constant source of motivation. A weakness of the theory is that it lacked hard evidence to support it. Also, because different people have different priorities at different times in their lives the idea of a steady progression up a rigid hierarchy is difficult to accept. The application of the theory to training and work is difficult as many employees may be able to satisfy some of the higher needs outside of work. For example, a junior clerk may not be highly motivated at work because they have achieved recognition outside work in other activities they regard more highly and in which they are motivated, e.g. sports or politics. Indeed, a number of talented individuals may seek a modest position at work for fear that further career progression may limit their ability to be involved in activities outside the workplace.

Want to know more?

Sunday Times Best companies to work for:
www.bestcompanies.co.uk/list_mechanics.htm

A variation on needs theory was provided by F W Herzberg in 1957. Using interviews with accountants and engineers Herzberg and his colleagues arrived at a two-factor model of motivation related to different sets of needs. The two sets of motivators as described by Herzberg are:

- **Intrinsic motivators** – these relate to motivation that comes from within an individual or the work that they do, the quality of working life. The intrinsic motivators include personal development through responsibility, application of skills, freedom of action and deriving satisfaction from the challenges of the work environment.
- **Extrinsic motivators** – these come from outside the individual or the work itself but have a motivating effect. Pay, praise, punishment and promotion would come into this category along with status.

Intrinsic motivators were also referred to as 'satisfiers' and extrinsic motivators were termed 'dissatisfiers'. Satisfiers or intrinsic motivators were, concluded Herzberg, more likely to lead to improved performance and effort over the longer term. Dissatisfiers referred to the external environment of the individual and had a positive short-term impact. Dissatisfiers had little effect on attitudes, although employers needed to try to satisfy these motivators in order to maintain performance and prevent a decline in job performance. As dissatisfiers related to the external environment and were essentially preventative in nature, the term 'hygiene factors' was applied to them.

Herzberg's conclusions have been criticised in failing to establish a link between satisfaction and performance and for drawing wide conclusions from a limited number of interviews, just over 200, with a narrow range of occupations.

 McClelland's, McGregor's and Bennis's views of motivation and leadership, pages 54, 56, 57

ⒸASE STUDY

Capita offices are an oasis

In December Capita opened a Bristol call centre for TV licensing staff, fitted with improved work areas and oasis zones where staff can take breaks. Call centres are known as fairly stressful places to work. Paul Stanfield, call centre manager for the Bristol office, said: 'There has been a lot of research that shows it's good to get away from your desk and socialise, so we provide a breakout area on each floor.'

The areas contain snack machines, coffee machines, fridges, microwaves and TVs. They are also designed to appeal to the senses. Stanfield said: 'There are planters and water features, and each area is colour coded. So one is green, which is a reviving colour, one is red, one purple and so on.'

The work areas have also been redesigned to offer a more pleasant environment.

Stanfield said: 'It's important to show people we've invested in them. It gives people pride in what they do and pride in the company.'

http://www.employeebenefits.co.uk/News/Default.asp

ACTIVITY

By what other names are intrinsic and extrinsic motivators known?

The implications of Herzberg's work are nonetheless clear. Simply put, pay and working conditions need to be acceptable to maintain minimum levels of work performance but improved performance can only be sustained if work is designed in such a way as to be stimulating and in line with individuals' interests and skills.

CASE STUDY

Interview – Cary Cooper

Cary Cooper is professor of organisational psychology at the Manchester School of Management at UMIST. Cooper believes that in the past 20 years Britain has developed American-style management, and a corresponding workplace: 'The UK has a long working hours culture, intrinsic job insecurity, lack of work/life balance, and much more robust and abrasive management styles.' He concludes that the number one issue for employee motivation is work/life balance. 'It is a very, very significant benefit. They want to be given autonomy, to be able to do their job to meet their objectives. But they want to be able to do it at the time that is convenient for them, in their personal lives, and the place that is convenient for them.'

Flexible working also helps people feel in control. Cooper explains: 'Companies that want people at their desk all the time are seen as untrusting organisations. These employers don't understand employees can work from home and be effective.' He believes that a good employer is one who says, 'Here are the objectives that you have to achieve; where you achieve them from, when you do it and how you do it is up to you. We trust you.' He emphasises the need to use a management style that balances reward and punishment. 'Everybody in the workplace knows that if they make mistakes they are going to be told they have made a mistake, they expect that. But they don't get much praise when they do things right. Having a manager who values what they do is an important indirect benefit.' Cooper thinks organisations lose out when they fail to consider their employees' outside lives. 'People live very complex lives outside work. What may appear as a demotivated person, may just be someone who is stressed by something that's going on in his personal life.' Cooper feels understanding employees is key to formulating a motivation strategy. Unfortunately Cooper does not believe the majority of UK organisations look at motivation this strategically. He believes this training is particularly key for lower-level supervisors. 'A lot of these people get to supervisory jobs on the basis of technical skill. If we are going to do motivational training, the people who need it the most are those people.' He cites the case of an organisation which did this with its shop floor workers. 'At the end of it they said it was a double benefit. Number one, they were exposed to stuff they are never normally exposed to, and, number two, they felt valued.' Cooper believes most employees and their managers are intrinsically motivated. 'Some are motivated by fear of job loss, some are motivated by being given the mobility they want to get a better job or better quality of life.' Not all employees are brimming with motivation, but Cooper believes this isn't necessarily a problem. 'As long as they are doing a good job and that is all they want to do, why not just accept it?'

Based on an article at
http://www.employeebenefits.co.uk/News/Default.asp

CTIVITY

List the following incentives and say whether they are intrinsic or extrinsic motivators:

- salary
- bonus
- promotion
- training
- career development
- praise
- autonomy
- shared ownership
- responsibility
- having your pay docked for being late
- threat of redundancies.

Explain your answers.

Applying the theories to work

How motivation theories are applied will depend on the assumptions managers make about the nature of their employees. E H Schein puts forward four models of 'man' to describe how employees may be depicted:

- **Rational-economic** – this view sees staff as mainly motivated by their rational logical understanding of their economic needs.
- **Social** – the social view sees staff as being mainly influenced by group influences and the need for rewarding interpersonal relationships.

- **Self actualising** – the self actualising view sees the opportunity to be independent and responsible for their own work as a critical motivator for individuals.
- **Complex** – this approach rejects any one of the previous three and depicts people as a complex mixture of all characteristics who satisfy their needs away from work as well as in work.

In an effort to get managers in the late 1950s and early 1960s to think about how they viewed their employees D McGregor put forward the Theory X and the Theory Y views.

McGregor was attempting to show mangers that a range of approaches was possible and was not advocating a particular management style as he is sometimes misinterpreted as having meant.

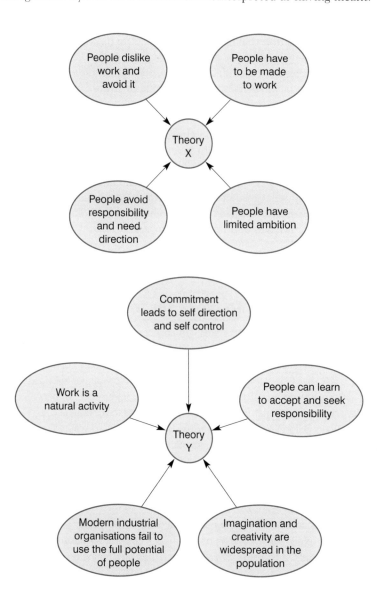

Figure 10 *Theory X and Theory Y put forward extreme views of worker behaviour*

Douglas McGregor,
page 56

He was attempting to highlight the need for the organisation to reconcile the needs of the individual with the needs of the workplace.

Hackman and Oldham in 1976 put forward several key aspects that should be considered in the process of work design. These were:

- **Skill variety** – employees should have a variety of tasks
- **Task identity** – employees should be free to decide what tasks to do and in what order, so long as work was satisfactorily completed
- **Task significance** – employees should understand that their work was important in the production process.

This degree of freedom of action and recognition, coupled with feedback about how well they were doing, would motivate employees and lead to good quality work where employees had a high degree of satisfaction resulting in low absenteeism and staff turnover rates.

In practice firms approach issues of motivation differently. Some firms will provide recognition to employees with separate dining areas for employees of a particular grade and different dress codes. Other firms, particularly Japanese car manufacturers, ensure that staff dress the same and use the same facilities irrespective of grade or status. At fastfood chain McDonalds, staff have badges with stars, each star recognising a step in their development and training; the army uses shoulder stripes and badges to denote rank. On some production lines employees may be discouraged from talking, in others talking might be encouraged. Reserved car parking spaces are used in some organisations to reflect the importance of certain jobs while employees at lower levels have no such benefit. We are able to learn a little about what assumptions are being made about workers and the sort of motivation strategies that are being used by looking at the way firms organise themselves and reward employees.

CASE STUDY

Best company to work for in 2003

Microsoft and its founder, Bill Gates, the richest man on the planet, certainly have their enemies. But among the fans are 1,595 employees whose sense of wellbeing and belief have taken the firm from second place last year to top our poll for the best company to work for in Britain.

When Maxine Edwards, who as 'readiness programme manager' prepares staff to launch new products, was called to a breakfast meeting in Oxfordshire her heart sank. But she and hard-worked colleagues were surprised with a 'thank you' stay at a luxury hotel. 'We work long hours but it doesn't feel like work most of the time: it is cool stuff and very upbeat,' she says. 'One of our directors sent an e-mail saying he doesn't want to see us after 6 pm. I've never heard of anything like that before.'

Microsoft has got one programme spot on: the way it treats its workforce. In our survey, it is the only company in which staff feel more strongly about the business as a whole than their own teams or managers.

The top score, 93% of staff, feel proud to work for the company and say it 'makes a positive difference to the world we live in'; 92% are excited about where it is going and would miss it if they left. About nine in 10 praise Microsoft's positive and faith-inspiring leadership, together with its high regard for customers, and 89% say they love working there.

The headquarters in Reading is spectacular, with a lake where charity rowing teams train, a forest and picnic tables.

As well as a Wellbeing clinic, offering everything from a mechanical massage chair to well-man clinics (including classes on how to detect testicular cancer), there is a 'bump' club to help pregnant mothers before their 18 weeks' fully paid leave, on-site nurses and doctor, and even a facility to donate bone marrow.

The firm has opened a crèche with 50 places for £35 a day (£37 for the under-2s), has four cafés, a subsidised restaurant and Xbox games terminals for entertainment (if television stations including the own-brand UTV are not enough). Sports are given a boost with a £260,000 social budget, and the firm subsidises outings to shows or trips abroad.

Although staff say the firm is not the top payer in the industry, two-thirds earn more than £40,000 a year while 95% have joined a sharesave scheme with 15% off.

There is free private healthcare (including 'life partners' and family), and a four-month sabbatical (unpaid) after four years. Flexible options to be introduced this year include dental cover, childcare vouchers for staff in London and Edinburgh and for those working from home, and the chance to buy days off.

Source: Based on an article from Sunday Times Best Companies to Work For list at www.bestcompanies.co.uk/list

Groups at work

Upon the efforts of each depends the fate of all.

Alexander The Great

It is clear from the previous section that social interaction at work is a critical component of work design. It is for this reason that many businesses make use of a group or team approach to work. Group work is particularly useful in:

- dealing with unfamiliar problems for which no set procedure exists in the organisation, and/or
- where a wide range of skills is needed, and/or
- managers are seeking to gain employee commitment to whatever course of action is decided.

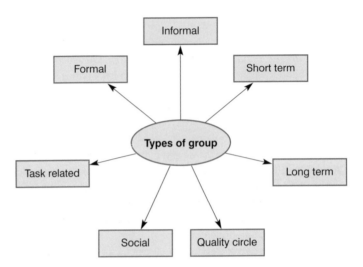

Figure 11 Work groups exist for a
variety of purposes

CASE STUDY

Team work

Ever feel like your team is getting nowhere fast? Teamwork can be an excellent way for colleagues to use their shared knowledge to problem solve and create products or solutions. However, it's important to determine whether forming a team will enhance your company's productivity on a project or just waste valuable resources.

If you're thinking teamwork is the way to go, ask yourself the following questions before you round up the troops and get the project underway.

Are you sure you need a team to do the job?

Sometimes, assigning a team to a project just isn't the best choice. Some jobs will be completed more efficiently if assigned to one person. If an individual has the knowledge, time and experience to fly solo on a project, let them. That will leave more people free for projects that really need a team approach.

Does a team have enough time to do the job right?

There is nothing worse than wasting people's valuable time with undefined goals. Tell your team what you want them to accomplish and why this job is important to the company. Otherwise, it's difficult for people to give their all to a project they consider meaningless.

Before you create your team, know what their exact task will be. Having a common objective will keep team members motivated. It's also wise to give team members a clear picture of what role each individual will play.

Does the team know exactly what they need to accomplish?

Team members should have a reasonable amount of time to work together and achieve their goal. Rushing a team will cut down on productivity because of increased pressure and lack of time to come up with the creative results your company craves.

Establish a clear start and finish date at the beginning of the project. The team may disagree and request a new target date, but at least you'll know ahead of time instead of facing last-minute requests for deadline extensions.

Have you picked the right people?

Look for team members who are open to new ideas and supportive of one another.

Build your team from people who can cover all aspects of the project. When feasible, have people from different departments on your team – marketing, accounting, even the mailroom. Ten heads may be better than one, but not if they all think exactly the same way. The job will get done faster when the necessary information and resources are encompassed within the team members.

But remember that no one is perfect. People have different ways of approaching projects, and teamwork sometimes results in disagreements. To help team members get over obstacles and maintain productivity assign a team facilitator.

If you're creating the team for the right reasons and taking the time to set up a diverse group, you'll be sure to see increased productivity on all your team endeavours.

Source: Business Week, 27 November 2000. Based on article at
http://www.effectivemeetings.com/teams/index.asp

CTIVITY

What circumstances or tasks would be unsuitable for a group work approach to a task or problem?

Management styles,
page 59

Types of group

Groups have different characteristics, which will be affected by the overall management style of the organisation, the tasks they have to complete and the time that they have to complete their tasks. The individuals who are members of the group will affect its running by the way in which they interact. Mangers responsible for bringing a group or team together need to have regard therefore to the management style, tasks, time and personalities involved.

Short-term groups

These are groups that are brought together to complete a particular task or for a particular period of time. Normally the group will break up once the task or project is completed or the time period has elapsed.

Long-term groups

These groups tend to be part of the normal work structure. They could, for example, be a group involved in specialist parts of the production process such as research, or carry out a wider range of duties, such as in a word-processing pool.

Formal groups

A formal group could be short term or long term. The size and membership of a formal group will be determined by the tasks for which it is responsible. Normally the group will have specific tasks to carry out and its membership will be made up of individuals with the necessary skills to ensure the goals are met. The leader will be clearly identified and group members will have clear tasks and responsibilities. Notes of meetings will normally be kept and, commonly, circulated to managers and others who are outside the group so that they can be aware of developments and decisions. In a formal setting the notes of the meeting may be passed on to another group. For example, a school or college governing body may have a subcommittee responsible for financial affairs. Usually the notes of this group's meetings will be passed on to the full governing body.

Informal group

This type of group is usually made up of people with a common interest. Because it is informal, the group's membership can change as relations between its members change and develop. An informal group could be short term or long term. Such groups may not be recognised by the formal structure of the organisation but their discussions and information sharing can help the work of the organisation, although informal groups tend to operate in the interests of the individual members. Informal groups tend not to record their decision making and do not formally report their work.

Task-related groups

These are similar in many ways to short-term groups. The life of the group is linked to particular tasks or projects and ends when these have been completed. Projects can involve researching or designing a new product, organising an office move or seeking external recognition such as an Investors In People award (IIP)

 Investors in People, page 77

Social groups

Social groups are important in an organisation as they serve as an alternative source of communication and support for group members. By their nature these groups are informal although they may, in some circumstances, organise events and activities for themselves and other members of the workforce. When this stage is reached some degree of formal organisation is required and the group has the characteristics of a task-related group.

Quality circles

Improvements in communication and technology mean that the differences between competitive products and services are no longer significant and competitive advantage soon tends to be eroded. One way many firms are seeking to gain a competitive edge is through improved quality and reliability. For these reasons quality circles deserve a specific mention, even though they have the characteristics of long-term, task-related formal groups. Quality circles involve regular meetings of around 5–10 volunteers engaged in similar tasks, under the leadership of their supervisor who, ideally, has been trained to lead these sessions. These meetings discuss and analyse various aspects of production, e.g. output, accidents, materials, equipment and organisation. Where problems are identified the group make recommendations about solutions to their management. Where approval is given the solutions are likely to be well implemented as the process has allowed the employees to participate in decisions about their own work and so has resulted in improved motivation.

Membership of quality circles can help develop employees' management and leadership skills and bring wider benefits. The voluntary nature of such schemes means that there is a risk that they fade away after an initial period of enthusiasm. Car manufacturers such as Nissan and Volvo have made use of quality circles in the past.

Generally group work can aid employee motivation through encouraging participation in the work process. A disadvantage of such an approach is that decision making and communication can be slower than a less participative approach.

Want to know more?

For general information and approaches to team building from a particular perspective look at www.teams.org.uk

Developing groups

Individuals who identify with their group are more likely to participate fully in the work of the group. Group identity is more likely if members like or respect each other and agree with the aims of the group. Tuckerman in 1965 identified the stages involved in developing a group as:

- Forming
- Storming
- Norming
- Performing.

There is no prescribed time limit over when these reactions will be witnessed. The extent to which they become evident, if at all, depends on the group leader, how group tasks are described and the nature of the individuals involved.

Forming

This involves members of the group starting to gain an understanding of what they are required to do and how they can behave. Great reliance is placed on the group leader to guide members through this stage.

Storming

As members become more confident of their role there will be a degree of resistance and challenging of the nature of the tasks they face. The conflict associated with this stage of development can lead to opposition to the leader.

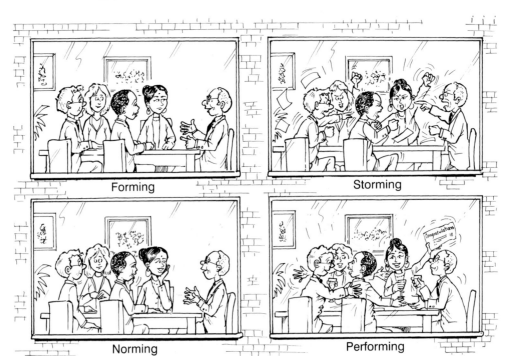

*Figure 12 Group
formation is a
challenging process*

Norming

The outcome of 'storming', assuming the group remains intact, is that group members gain a greater understanding of the tasks, themselves, and each other, as well as what is and isn't acceptable. This means that 'norms' have emerged. The emergence of norms results in better support, and communication leading to a sense of group identity.

Performing

The improved understanding that group members have at this stage means that they are able to work in a flexible, more trusting way. Energy is now devoted to the tasks in hand and the group can perform the work it is required to do.

ACTIVITY

Consider a situation you have been in that most closely related to Tuckerman's forming, storming, norming and performing model and describe it to others. What were the main areas of conflict at the storming stage and how were these resolved?

Conflict resolution

Team working is not always successful or easy. Conflict within or between teams is usually to blame for lack of success.

Conflict within teams

Conflict within the team can be the result of several factors:
- Domination by the team leader or one or two other team members
- Members fail to complete tasks or leave others to do the work
- Personality clashes unrelated to the work
- Failure to understand or explain the purpose of the team and required outcomes
- Team members lack good listening skills
- Team members are not prepared to give and take.

Effective training, preparation and communication can avoid many of the pitfalls that stop good group work. An understanding of the roles that group members could play is also important.

R F Bales conducted a series of observations of small group interaction and the published results of this research in 1950 indicated that successful groups had to have members that were effective in both social and emotional terms as well as in terms of the task they were working on. Positive social and emotional responses included supporting others, raising the status of others, humour, agreement and complying with decisions. Positive task-related behaviour involved putting forward suggestions, guiding others, sharing information and offering an opinion.

One of the most popular models of team membership is that developed by Belbin in 1981. Belbin identified eight roles that are needed within a team, if it is to succeed. Personality tests are available to help individuals identify to which of these roles their normal behaviour most closely relates. The roles are described in Figure 14.

- Company worker – characterised by keeping the interests of the business at the forefront of discussion
- Chairman – offers direction and ensures others are heard
- Shaper – takes the views of several people and shapes them together, helping a shared view to emerge about the way the team should work
- Plant/ideas person – tends to put forward the ideas and strategy, often quite creative
- Resource investigator – checks the viability of ideas in relation to the available resources and the situation outside the team
- Monitor-evaluator – tests and evaluates the ideas being put forward and offers comments
- Team worker – this person assists the social cohesion or team spirit of the group in ways that can include humour and improved communication
- Completer-finisher – this person focuses on completing the task in hand with a view to a successful outcome and attempts to keep the group on course for completion.

Every individual has elements of all of these team roles within them. How they play them depends on many factors, including a person's confidence and commitment. Although we have aspects of these roles

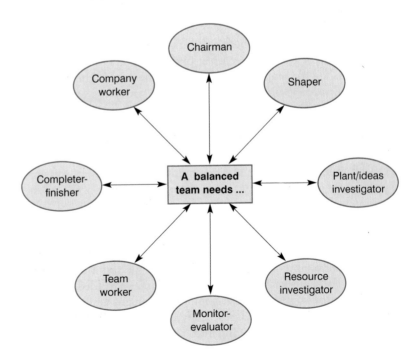

Figure 13 Belbin's team roles model
helps us understand how team
members might interact

within us, personality testing indicates that some tend more towards one or two of these roles than others. The skill of a manager in assembling a team is to ensure it has the necessary range of skills and commitment to complete the task on time and within budget to a good standard.

**CTIVITY**

Consider the individuals in your group. Without discussion with others, classify them according to Belbin's team role model. Compare your notes with others and consider why your answers were as similar or as different as they were.

Want to know more?

To find out more about Meredith Belbin visit www.sol.brunel.ac.uk/~jarvis/bola/teams/belbin2.html

Conflict between teams

As well as potential conflict within groups, in a workplace that features several, group conflict between groups is a possibility. This inter-group conflict can arise for several reasons:

- **Poor communication** – groups in conflict might have different priorities or lack developed communication skills
- **Poor co-ordination of inter-related processes** – conflicting groups might be working on inter-related tasks and poor co-ordination can lead to delays or lack of time to complete work
- **Problems in the design of the organisation** – the structure of the organisation, particularly one on several sites, may make it difficult for members of conflicting groups to exchange ideas and information
- **Perceived unfair distribution of resources** – the perception that one group is being treated more favourably than another, perhaps in terms of bonus or allocation of staff, can lead to conflict
- **Poor motivational technique** – where supervisors or managers are not skilled in motivating staff this can cause negative views about other work groups.

How inter-group conflict is resolved will vary according to the organisation's culture, financial health, use of technology and the needs of the individuals concerned. Possible approaches include the following.

- Reduce task interdependence between the groups and create adequately resourced self contained groups.
- Clarify responsibilities of groups and individuals and ensure these are observed.

- Sensitivity training. This is a high-risk, controversial approach whereby those in conflict are brought together and left to resolve the problem themselves. Minimal outside intervention is involved but where it occurs it needs to be sensible, sensitive and focused.
- Structured interaction. Bringing together those parties in conflict in a structured way that is skilfully led can help them identify, analyse and resolve their differences, often entailing a degree of compromise. Bringing people together in this way not only helps challenge stereotypes and misrepresentations but avoids some of the more sensitive, and potentially destructive, issues that arise in less structured approaches such as sensitivity training.
- Ignore it and hope it goes away. This is not recommended but is sometimes effective in dealing with minor issues and preventing them from escalating.
- Protracted discussions. Drawing out a discussion of the problem over a period of days, weeks or months can allow tempers to cool and rational thought to be restored.

Final thoughts

Conflict is generally thought of as a negative feature of business life. It can bring about business benefits, if skilfully managed, as the following table shows.

Constructive effect of conflict	Destructive effect of conflict
Produce different solutions to a problem	Divert attention from the objectives of the group
Clarify power relationships	Force people further apart
Encourage creativity	Limit creativity through blocking behaviour
Focus on individual contributions	Cause the group to disintegrate
Bring into the open non-rational arguments	Allow emotion to take over from rational decision making
Release of long-standing tensions	Provide the basis for future conflict

Based on J Hunt, *Managing People at Work*, Pan Books, London 1979

Table 1 Conflict can have a destructive or constructive impact

Styles of management

You don't manage people; you manage things. You lead people.
Admiral Grace Hooper

How an organisation approaches the issue of training, or any other aspect of its work such as sales or production, will be determined by its approaches to managing itself. Management is a frequently misunderstood term. The most well known definition is probably one used by Mary Parker Follet who said that management was 'The art of getting things done through people'. In other words, management is the organisation of the resources businesses use to provide their goods and services to customers.

In addition to being able to make decisions that further the aims of the business, managers need to be able to motivate the staff for whom they are responsible. In order to do these things managers need to understand how groups work and what motivates individuals in their team. How managers deal with their staff and look after their welfare will affect staff morale and motivation and, consequently, their performance.

> **Key term**
>
> **Management** – the art of getting things done through people.

 Motivation at work, page 33

 Groups at work, page 41

What makes a successful manager?

Managers should use a style of management that they think will bring success. Efforts have been made over the years to try to predict which people will make successful managers by trying to identify key features associated with successful managers. For example, S M Davies noted four factors, or personal traits, that contributed to the success of leaders:

- **Intelligence** – successful leaders tend to have a higher level of intelligence than their followers, it was argued
- **Social maturity** – successful leaders had the skill and confidence to deal with a range of situations
- **Goal focus** – the drive to achieve things and succeed was high in successful leaders
- **People skills** – effective leaders took an interest in their subordinates and developed a relationship with them.

Other approaches to understanding effective management have concentrated on the situation managers find themselves in, rather than personal characteristics or traits of the individual. For example, F E Fidler's contingency model of leadership effectiveness argued that the leader's effectiveness will be affected by:

- the state of relations between the leader and the team
- the extent to which subordinates' work is clearly defined
- how much formal authority the leader has over the group.

According to John Adair the extent to which managers will be successful will be determined by the extent to which they can balance three sets of needs in their work group:

- **Task needs** – in other words what needs to be done in order to complete the task
- **Team maintenance needs** – those things that helped the group to maintain and develop its sense of identify and continue to function
- **Individual needs** – the personal needs that members of the group had.

Ideally the effective manager's actions would have a positive effect on all three needs, or leadership functions, as Adair referred to them.

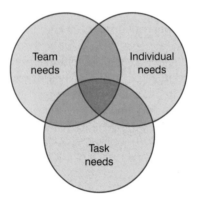

Figure 14 *The overlapping leadership
functions of Adair's leadership model*

The *Guardian* and *Observer* newspapers carry a range of business and management related articles on line at http://www.guardian.co.uk/

Ⓐ CTIVITY

Using the business supplements of Sunday newspapers such as the *Observer* or *Sunday Times* look at profiles of successful business leaders described on their pages. What characteristics, if any, do they have in common?

Management theorists

Management theorists are researchers whose study into the behaviour of workers and managers leads them to state a set of views – a theory – which, if generalised to the population as a whole, would provide guidance about how people behave at work. This could point managers and others towards decisions more likely to help them achieve their aims. The extent to which a person accepts a management theory as being accurate will be reflected in their approach to management, or their style of management, which we discuss below (page 59). Clearly, the better one's understanding of management theory, the better placed one will be to manage effectively, assuming a person has the other necessary personal skills.

Before discussing management styles, we consider some key management theorists and the ideas they put forward.

Key term
....
Management style – the approach used by a person to manage a situation.

Henri Fayol

Writing at the end of the nineteenth century and in the first half of the twentieth century, Fayol, a French industrialist, was one of the first management theorists. He saw management as having five activities. He said that 'to manage is to forecast and plan, to organise, to command, to co-ordinate and to control'. Most of the terms in his explanation are self-explanatory although the co-ordination aspect of a manager's role was, in Fayol's view, about the manager linking his or her responsibilities to those of others in the firm to harmonise activity and effort. The control part of Fayol's definition ensures that managers monitor the performance of the organisation against previously established targets and goals. Fayol focused on the administrative management of work rather than the detailed operational level of management.

Fredrick Winslow Taylor

F W Taylor was writing around the same time as Fayol but concentrated on the work of supervisors and managers. Taylor was a manager in the American steel industry who is best known for his theories of 'scientific management', which were first published in 1911. This approach attempted to increase managers' control of the work processes by giving them a better understanding of the work methods used by their staff so that output could be better co-ordinated and payment systems linked to employee performance to ensure greater co-operation and motivation. Taylor laid down four principles of scientific management that he felt would increase prosperity for workers and employees and reduce strikes and conflict in the workplace:

- **Develop a science of work**. A scientific approach to understanding what people were doing and what they were supposed to do would allow managers to determine what were reasonable levels of pay and output.
- **Systematic selection and training**. When employing staff, Taylor argued that there should be efforts to compare the manager's understanding of the job with the skills the applicant had to offer. This could ensure that the best person for the job was appointed. Understanding what the job involved would allow managers to make training available to employees which would help them work better and increase their income.
- **Division of tasks**. Having developed an understanding of the work managers should allow the employees to get on with their set of tasks and make progress on their own.
- **Manager and employee co-operation**. This would ensure that the scientific understanding of the work was being correctly applied. The shared understanding of what is required should reduce conflict and increase output.

Taylor has been criticised for, in the process of systemising working practices, not considering the human aspects of the process. Further criticisms are that he viewed motivation as being solely financial and had

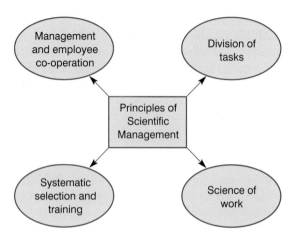

Figure 15 Taylor laid out the principles of scientific management

no regard to the other reasons why people work. The payment by results that arises from Taylor's approach meant that attention was focused on output and too little regard given to matters relating to the quality of the output. The focus on individuals that is a feature of Taylor's work had little regard for the roles of groups and the impact of group interaction. Taylor saw the social aspects of group work as a distraction and advocated breaking up work groups and re-forming them if needed, so as to minimise distractions. A further criticism is that by seeking to establish 'scientific principles' Taylor promoted the view that this approach would fit any situation. In fact there are some situations that are not suited to this approach and this led to costly mistakes.

Taylor's work demonstrated the benefits of a systematic approach to management issues and, like Fayol, much of what he put forward is accepted and used today.

**CTIVITY**

Consider a workplace with which you are familiar. What aspects of Fayol's and Taylor's approaches can you see in that workplace?

David McClelland

Based at Harvard University, McClelland's research led him to the view that people, or at least some of them, have a need to achieve. He understood this desire for achievement to be significantly a result of a childhood where parents had different expectations for their children relative to other parents and where they encouraged them to start acting independently at an early age. These achievement-minded people were characterised as being willing to work at a problem rather than leave the outcome to chance. They were prepared to take a moderate degree of risk in order to achieve their goal, but the achievement carried greater satisfaction than any monetary or other reward that might result. In other terms, they had a motivation similar to that described by Herzberg's hygiene motivation theory.

Money served as a measure of their success, not as the success itself. According to McClelland people who sought high achievement also sought regular concrete feedback on their performance. They tended to prefer information about what they had done, rather than general terms of praise or comments about personal characteristics.

A key outcome of McClelland's work was that where people were broadly of the same ability, those who were achievement-minded would tend to perform better in the same circumstances. Clearly businesses that can identify achievement-minded people or train them in the necessary skills could do well. McClelland devised training programmes to try to bring about increased desire for achievement. The research into the impact of these programmes is not conclusive and subject to some criticism, in that it was carried out by McClelland or his associates and that his work focused only on men and did not include women.

By the nature of their high levels of performance achievement-motivated people have greater opportunities to be promoted and become managers themselves. Their high level of focus on tasks and outcomes means that they run the risk of not considering the human or personal side of managing teams. This lack of patience can lead to their subordinates becoming frustrated or demotivated.

Herzberg's hygiene motivation theory, page 36

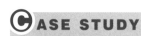

ASE STUDY

Who's in charge here? No one

Semco doesn't have a mission statement, its own rulebook or any written policies. It doesn't have an organisation chart, a human resources department or even, these days, a headquarters. Subordinates choose their managers, decide how much they are paid and when they work. Meetings are voluntary, and two seats at board meetings are open to the first employees who turn up. Salaries are made public, and so is all the company's financial information. Six months is the farthest ahead the group ever looks. Each half year its units decide how many people they require for the next half year period.

Sounds like a recipe for chaos, eh? Yet Semco has surfed Brazil's rough economic and political currents, often growing at between 30 and 40 per cent a year. It turns over $160 million, up from $4m when Ricardo Semler joined the family business two decades ago, and it employs 3,000. $100,000 invested in this barmy firm 20 years ago would now be worth $5m.

Semler argues that the reason for Semco's sustainability is the same one that makes conventional managers reject it: no one is in control, including Semler the major shareholder. The company recently held a party to commemorate the tenth anniversary of the last time he made any decision at all.

Semco is a test case of what happens when a company puts the annual report-speak of 'trust' and 'delegation' into practice. The result of democracy and treating people as adults – the only real rules at Semco – is huge peer pressure and self-discipline.

'It's as free market as we can make it. People bring their talents and we rely on their self-interest to use the company to develop themselves in any way they see fit,' declares Semler. 'In return, they must have the self-discipline to perform.'

There's no hiding place for those that don't, even if performance is judged in non-standard ways. 'To survive here you have to get on someone's list of people they need for the next six months, and you can't do that by playing political games.'

But conventional control attitudes are deeply programmed, and resistance to pursuing democratic logic, particularly at the bottom, is vicious. 'Even now,' laments Semler, 'we're only 50 or 60 per cent where we'd like to be'. Hence the constant attempts to unsettle even Semco's unusual order – the latest of which is the disbandment of the firm's headquarters in favour of satellite 'airport lounge' offices dotted around Sao Paulo. Not only do people not have fixed desks, they don't even have fixed offices.

'They thought it was about location. In fact, it's about eliminating control,' says Semler happily. 'If you don't even know where people are, you can't possibly keep an eye on them. All that's left to judge on is performance.'

Source: Based on an article in the Observer, 27 April 2003
http://www.observer.co.uk/business/story/0,6903,944138,00.html
© Simon Caulkin

Douglas McGregor

In order to promote a debate about how managers view their employees, McGregor put forward two contrasting views of workers. These were the Theory X and Theory Y approaches for which he is most well known. The Theory X view of employees was that they disliked work and sought to avoid it wherever possible. This meant that close control and direction was needed, backed up by threats of punishment to ensure sufficient effort was produced. People, according to the Theory X view, preferred to be directed, did not want responsibility and had little ambition. With this approach little regard was paid to the needs of the individual and the focus was on work. Theory X has the risk of being a self-fulfilling prophecy. If workers act in accordance with this view and passively accept close supervision and direction they are proving the theory to be true. If employees resist this approach and seek more influence this also re-enforces the view that they are not committed to the aims of the organisation and so need close supervision and direction.

Theory Y was linked to Maslow's needs hierarchy. According to Theory Y the physical and mental effort associated with work was natural to humans who would work in proportion to the rewards they received. These would be either financial rewards, self actualising/fulfilment rewards or some combination of both. According to this view, people were prepared to accept responsibility and generally had high levels of imagination and creativity that were under-used in the workplace.

With the application of Theory X poor performance can be corrected, in theory, by better supervision and more direction. Under Theory Y poor performance can be addressed through a range of training methods and efforts to address the needs of the individual.

McGregor argues that management by objectives, i.e. negotiation and agreement about what is to be done, is more productive than management by direction, where the supervisor or manager instructs the subordinate what to do with little or no regard for their views.

The Theory X and Theory Y approach has been mistakenly criticised for simplifying a view of management–worker relations – this was McGregor's intention in order to spark a debate. Another criticism is that his approach, like Maslow, overplays the importance of work in most people's lives.

 Maslow's hierarchy of needs, page 35

 Training methods, page 24

**CTIVITY**

In your experience which is the more accurate, Theory X or Theory Y?

Warren Bennis

Bennis studied and worked with Douglas McGregor after the second world war and continued producing stimulating work well into the 1990s, and he has a continuing influence on management theory. In his book *Leaders*, based on a study of 90 successful leaders such as Ray Kroc of McDonalds, Neal Armstrong the astronaut and various others including orchestral conductors and sports coaches, Bennis argued that:

- leadership was not a rare skill – most people can do it
- leaders were trained – not born
- people in all parts of the organisation were leaders – not just those at the top
- leadership was about giving people the power to do things rather than controlling and directing them.

Of the leaders he studied Bennis argued that they had four things in common.

Vision

Successful managers had a clear view of what they wanted the organisation to be doing in the future, how it would do it and what the benefits would be for all concerned. This vision was motivational and drew the attention and support of others in the organisation who could see where they fitted into the future of the organisation. Achieving the vision was the focus of the activity of the group. Vision was linked to the second factor.

Communication

Methods of communication, page 66

The communication of the vision involved conveying optimism and trust by a variety of means that got over the message and the vision for the future clearly to the target audience. The best leaders were also good listeners who sought the advice of a variety of people inside and outside their organisation using both formal and informal methods of communication. Using their communications as a way of constantly learning, the leaders attempted to make their organisations 'responsible communities' where a group of interdependent people worked and learned together for the common good. The effect of good communication was not only to help people understand the vision for the organisation but to develop a commitment to achieving the vision from all concerned. The commitment involved changing the way the organisation and individuals worked in order to better implement the vision.

Trust

This, according to Bennis, is 'the emotional glue that binds followers and leaders together'. Trust was achieved by leaders acting consistently and setting out a vision that others understood and found clear, attractive and attainable. By knowing where the leader stood in relation to internal and external issues followers were able to work and plan in a consistent framework.

Positive self regard

The successful leaders in Bennis's study felt good about themselves. As a result they were able to accept other people as they were and in a courteous manner. In their dealings with people leaders concentrated on the present, not the past, which avoided overemphasis on past errors but in a way that allowed these to be learned from by dealing with the current results. Good leaders did not allow their familiarity with colleagues to stop them listening to what they had to say, and they avoided taking their colleagues for granted. Effective leaders trusted people, even when this appeared something of a risk, but at the same time did not rely on the approval of others to judge their own performance. This emotional wisdom meant they did not seek to be a 'good guy' but to produce good quality and effective results.

Positive self regard meant that the good leaders, while prepared to examine their weaknesses in order to learn and improve, focused on their, and their organisation's, strengths. Bennis demonstrates this point with reference to Karl Wallenda, a famous tightrope walker. Prior to a walk in 1978 over a 75 feet drop, Wallenda had for some months been focusing on not falling. Before his other exploits he had concentrated on crossing the wire and planned how to do this. It is suggested that by concentrating on not falling, Wallenda was focusing on a negative outcome. This inevitably occurred when he fell to his death in what was to be his last walk.

Want to know more?

The Chartered Management Institute has a magazine (*Professional Manager*) and website devoted to management issues and related information at http://ocula.managers.org.uk

 **CTIVITY**

Which modern managers, politicians, business leaders or other public figures in your view show the characteristics of successful leaders that Bennis describes?

Management styles

Over the years many theories about management have developed and these have led to different ways of categorising styles of management. It should be recognised that these are descriptions of human behaviour and, as such, are only rough guides to the way people act. The management style an individual may use will be affected by several factors such as their age, education, customs and rules of the business they are in and their own personal philosophy.

While the categories, or models, of management described here are only approximations of how people behave, an understanding of management styles helps people to develop their own approach and understand the behaviour of others. A selection of management styles includes the following.

Autocratic

The autocratic manager rarely delegates or shares information with subordinates. This type of manager draws on their status and power to direct subordinates and is resistant to any challenge to their way of doing things. The standards of others required by an autocratic manager are fixed and not subject to negotiation. Many subordinates subject to this approach can feel excluded from decision making and control over their own work, which leads to feelings of frustration and resentment, characterised by low motivation. This 'top down' approach leads to subordinates relying on the manager for direction whenever problems or unusual developments occur. This dependence re-enforces the autocratic control of the manager. This style generally stifles creativity and initiative in the work team.

Democratic

The democratic manager involves staff in decision making and tends to follow the majority view in setting standards and targets. This type of manager does little to re-enforce discipline or rules, believing that, having involved staff in establishing group targets and standards, the group members will implement their decisions and stick to the rules. Where workers are well motivated and quite able they may be willing to engage with this approach, which can lead to good performance. Less able or less well motivated workers will find the lack of guidance frustrating. The requirement to participate in decisions that are not directly part of their job will prove irritating for these workers, who may not engage fully with it and therefore not feel committed to abiding by the rules and targets for the group.

Laissez-faire

Translated from the French this means, broadly, 'to do as you like'. As the term suggests, managers leave members largely to their own devices, even to the extent of identifying what they will do, when they will do it and how. For highly able and well motivated individuals this approach can be stimulating, increase motivation and lead to high standards and good levels of output. However, where individuals rely on others for aspects of their work this approach can result in poor co-ordination, hold-ups in production and frustration. Poorly motivated staff are unlikely to be at their most productive with the low levels of supervision associated with this approach, while many less able employees will find the lack of guidance and support uncomfortable and work less efficiently in the absence of adequate guidance and supervision.

Contingency

Managers who follow this approach reject the idea that one style of management can fit the variety of situations they have to deal with. Managers who adopt this approach try to obtain a fit between the organisation or department's goals and strategy, employee needs and the pressure it faces from the external environment. In practice this means that the contingent manager will have regard for a variety of issues and choose what they consider to be the correct approach to a given situation. If, for example, the demands of a problem require them to be autocratic and directive they will be; if the chances of reaching the best goal for all concerned is through a more democratic approach this is the approach they will adopt. For the contingent approach to work well, and to avoid demotivating employees by what they might see as inconsistent behaviour, managers need to communicate effectively to ensure that staff understand the broad aims of the organisation and are adequately supervised and supported but without stifling innovation or creativity. Adair and Fiedler are proponents of this approach to management.

Task-based

Task-based management can be, to some degree, associated with the laissez-faire approach. This approach works by bringing together individuals with the necessary range of skills and understanding to deal with a task that is necessary to carry forward the aims of the business. Unlike the autocratic approach, this approach places little reliance on managers for guidance and supervision but rests on the employees involved being sufficiently knowledgeable and committed to complete the task to which they are assigned. This approach is unlikely to work in circumstances where tasks require little skill and tend to be repetitive. Work involving complex uncommon tasks and a highly skilled workforce is better suited to this sort of approach.

 Teams, groups and tasks, page 42

Situational

A situational approach to management is linked to theories about traits. In other words, businesses that use this approach believe that there are certain personal characteristics in a manager that are better suited to particular situations. Situationalist approaches reject the idea of traditional trait approaches that there is one set of personal traits that make a good manager in any circumstances; instead they propose that some personal qualities are better suited to deal with particular circumstances than others. Businesses that take this approach will deploy managers and staff into situations where they believe their personalities, skills and knowledge will best suit the needs of the business. Critics of this approach argue that the advantages gained from the unique characteristics or knowledge of a manager deployed in this way will gradually fade as others become familiar with the situation and the manager concerned.

Pro-active

If a management style is pro-active it means that it involves the manager actively trying to anticipate problems and situations that can be improved upon to the benefit of the organisation. Pro-active management can be combined with any of the types listed above but is characterised by good communications between the manager, colleagues and sub-ordinates and a good understanding of the external influences that affect their business. By bringing together good external awareness and good communication networks inside the business the pro-active manager can not only anticipate problems and opportunities but also mobilise the skills and support needed to deal with them to the benefit of the business. Change is recognised by the pro-active manager to be a continuous part of the process of their day-to-day business activity.

Reactive

The characteristics of a reactive management style are broadly the opposite of the pro-active style. Similarly, reactive management approaches can be linked to any of the styles listed above. Reactive managers tend to focus on the defined tasks and responsibilities. They may often be very good at what they do and have good relationships with their team and achieve to a good level. The inability to anticipate developments means that changes in circumstances often find them poorly prepared since they have committed ideas and resources to dealing with their day-to-day responsibilities. Change can be disruptive for reactive managers and their teams and seen as a disruptive event, rather than part of a constant process. This perception means that change is often a more stressful experience for reactive managers and their teams than for proactive managers and their subordinates.

CASE STUDY

Eye for minutiae

Every office has one. The boss who's a bit of a control freak – always looking over people's shoulders, monitoring their every move, checking even tiny, insignificant pieces of work.

If you've had to work for one of these 'micro-managers' you'll know just how frustrating and demoralising an experience it can be. Left unchecked, micro-management can spread through the organisation like a virus, knocking motivation and morale for six and crushing creativity and innovation in its wake.

So how does it happen – and what can be done to stop the rot? Organisational psychologist Bruce Katcher suggests that sometimes the problem starts at the top. 'The CEO or president micro-manages his or her own staff; the staff then unconsciously adopt the same management style with their direct reports. The practice spreads throughout the organisation and becomes part of the culture,' he explains.

Middle managers who have worked their way up through the ranks can be culprits too. They often struggle with the demands of a new management role and retreat into their comfort zone, spending their time on familiar tasks making themselves feel productive.

Poor recruitment practices are a problem. Not considering future needs means organisations recruit people who can do the job now – rather than those who can take the business into the future. If line managers lack interviewing skills, they risk hiring incompetent people, who they will then be forced to micro-manage!

'If people can let go of some of the reactive stuff and become more pro-active in terms of thinking strategically, planning and coaching, then that is what moves the organisation on,' says Margaret Gordon, senior consultant with Inspiring Performance. 'Progress only comes when you let go of the here and now and start thinking long term.'

Gordon suggests organisations need to look at the messages they give out about what kind of work is valued. 'There's a tendency to reward people for the reactive work and not the proactive work,' she says. 'You don't often hear people say "what a fantastic bit of planning", or "wow, what a crisis averted".'

'A lot of people are reluctant to delegate because they can't see where they would move onwards and upwards in the flatter structures. It's about protecting and keeping their own role,' says Gordon.

The rise of the blame culture may also be a factor. If people know they are going to be hanged, drawn and quartered if a project goes pear-shaped, they are likely to keep a very tight rein on it. 'It is possible to break out of this self-defeating cycle, but only if managers shift to a completely different mind-set,' says Malcolm Higgs of Henley Management College.

Experience from the BT Global Challenge round-the-world yacht race backs up a no-blame view. The crew on the winning yacht, LG Flatron, attributed much of their success to the fact that they agreed early on to create a no-blame culture.

'We always reviewed the things that went right rather than dwelling on the things that went wrong,' explained watch leader Laura Parrish. 'For example, if we did a good sail change we would talk about how we did it and analysed the detail because that is how you get better.'

Occupational psychologist Peter Honey stresses that this emphasis on coaching – rather than pointing the finger – is critical when your worst fears become reality and a delegated task goes horribly wrong.

Source: Based on an article in the online magazine of Professional Manager http://ocula.managers.org.uk (April 2003)

 **CTIVITY**

Copy out this table and put a tick in the box that represents the best style of management for the given situation. The first one is done for you.

Situation	Autocratic	Democratic	Laissez Faire	Contingency	Task Based
Leading soldiers	✓				
Managing a hospital					
Managing barristers					
Supervising a car production line					
Managing builders					
Self-employed plumber					

Communicating with the workforce

If you want to give a man credit, put it in writing. If you want to give him hell, do it on the phone.

Charles Beacham

Two monologues do not make a dialogue.

Jeff Daly

Previous sections on motivation and management have shown the importance of effective communication in the relationships between managers and other employees. Effective communication is particularly important in relation to training activity.

In H M Carlisle's definition, organisational communication is the use of systems to convey information to large numbers of people inside and outside the organisation. By contrast, interpersonal communication is communication between individuals to share information and understanding. According to H W Greenbaum, organisational communication has four main objectives:

- **Regulation** – ensuring employees conform to organisational instructions and requirements
- **Innovation** – to promote changes in the way operations are carried out
- **Integration** – developing a sense of identity in the workforce and raising morale
- **Information** – passing on factual details that people need in order to perform their organisational tasks.

These requirements are evident in the organisation's need to communicate about training or other business matters. Most communication in a business tends to be formal – in other words it follows the formal structure of the organisation. The amount of information and responsibility associated with individuals' communication will be linked to their place in the organisational structure.

 **CTIVITY**

How are the objectives of organisational and interpersonal communication different?

Informal communication, or the grapevine, does not follow formal structures but lines of social relationships and friendship groups instead. K Davis noted that the amount of informal communication grows when official, formal communication grows, as people discuss and analyse what they are being told formally. Rumour and gossip, which are not normally associated with the grapevine, were found to grow only in the absence of information from formal sources.

Internal communication strategy at British Aerospace plc

Employees: 46,600
Business: Commercial Aerospace and Defence
INVOLVING EVERYONE – employee communications

Business challenge

To assist business planning and execution of business plans in a rapidly changing competitive market and environment. The internal communication strategy makes appropriate use of a range of communication tools in order to provide context and clarity for individual job roles, objectives and day-to-day activity.

Issues and implications

A major staff opinion survey indicated that people's level of business awareness was low. It was important to get communication right, so that people could make the links between their own activity and that of the broader business and to help them understand how the organisation needed them to respond when market conditions change.

Learning

Information needed to be made readily available and simultaneously there needed to be a culture where the onus was on the individual 'pulling' this information from the various systems for themselves – as and when they needed it, rather than waiting for, or expecting it to be 'pushed' at them.

To achieve this, communication skills and techniques are included as corporate competencies.

People management initiatives and options

There is a common framework for communication throughout British Aerospace underpinned by a centrally produced core brief. The different business units are free to communicate the central messages in ways that work best for them. Team meetings are pre-scheduled a year ahead. Other communication tools and methods include:

- Electronic methods for urgent news.
- Every employee receives 'The Value Plan' – which outlines the annual business plan.
- Most senior managers use walkabouts and host events such as lunches.
- Notice boards – and themed posters for special campaigns – in the manufacturing areas.
- The bi-monthly journal 'Arrow', which covers broad based, company-wide information, and local house magazines.

- A magazine-style video programme, reporting on progress and performance, for all employees twice a year.
- A policy of open communication with the trade unions which takes place at twice-yearly meetings between the Chief Executive and the relevant senior union representatives.

Measurement and evaluation

The extent to which the objectives of the internal communication strategy are met is evaluated by auditing and through employee opinion surveys. Feedback questionnaires are used to ascertain views and reactions to such matters as the Value Plan and video programmes. The company also makes extensive use of focus groups to supplement the employee opinion surveys.

Business benefits

The company objectives and the plan as outlined in the 'Value Plan' document set minimum standards for communication across all the business units – which clarifies what all employees can expect.
Source: Based on a case study at http://www.greatplacetowork.gov.uk/

Methods of communication

The method of communication used by a manager will depend on who is being communicated with, the cost of the communication, the urgency of the communication, if a record of the message is required, how confidential the message is and who is sending it.

Communication happens in several ways. Table 2 outlines some of the main methods of communication.

Table 2 There are many methods of communication

Type of communication	Formal/ Organisational	Informal/ Interpersonal
Letter	*	
Corporate plans	*	
Memo	*	
Report	*	
Contract of employment/terms and conditions	*	
Notices		*
Induction programmes	*	
Appraisals	*	
Spoken (verbal communication)	*	*
Non-verbal communication	*	*
Meetings	*	*

Terms and conditions

The law (Employment Protection Act 1978) requires that an employer issue a Contract of Employment to new employees within 13 weeks of them starting work. The contract must outline the terms and conditions of employment, including:

- The rate of pay for the job in question and how payment is to be made, i.e. weekly or monthly, in cash or direct to a bank
- Hours to be worked
- Holiday arrangements and entitlement
- Arrangements for sick pay
- Length of notice to be worked
- Job title
- Grievance procedure – in other words what the employee is entitled to do if s/he feels unfairly treated.

The terms and conditions of employment set out what the employer expects of the employee and what the employee can expect in return for meeting their obligations.

Induction programme

It is common for most firms to arrange an induction programme for new employees. In the best cases this is planned and structured and takes place off the job. In the worst cases induction is unplanned and takes place on the job. The purpose of effective induction is to help new employees get used to the firm and its procedures and clarify their understanding of the terms and conditions of their employment. The programme should win their further commitment to the organisation and ensure that they are able to work productively from the earliest stage. The length of the induction period will vary. In some firms the induction programme might last only a morning, in others it might last a week. During the course of induction the new employee will normally find out about routine matters such as meal break times, company rules and what goods or services the firm provides. It is usual in large businesses for the employee to be told how they fit into the whole organisation and what their section of the organisation does. Many organisations will provide new employees with a handbook or booklet outlining rules and procedures with a description of the work of the business. This handbook will clarify the terms and conditions and inform staff about training and other facilities. Other matters covered in the induction period might be Health and Safety regulations, equality legislation and an introduction to the trade unions in the firm. A firm's induction programme will usually involve visits to different parts of the firm, as well as talks and lectures. Effective induction activity can be an important part of reducing staff turnover.

 **CTIVITY**

List the ways in which an induction programme could
(a) cost an organisation money, and
(b) save an organisation money.

Appraisal

Sometimes known as performance appraisal, the purpose of appraisal is to help workers be better at their jobs, to the benefit of both firm and worker. The process assesses employees against targets and expectations, gives feedback on their performance, allows an exchange of views to take place and establishes plans for further actions and improvements. Effective appraisal will re-enforce good performance and plan actions to eliminate weaker performance.

There are different methods of appraisal but they have several features in common. Appraisal involves an employee discussing their work with their manager. The employee might fill in a questionnaire before the appraisal interview and the questionnaire becomes the starting point of the discussion. Points often dealt with in any appraisal system might include how well the employee works with others, what they think their strengths and weaknesses are, what their career ambitions are and any ideas they have for improving the way their part of the firm works. It is usual for the manager to write a report of the discussion – sometimes this is in agreement with the employee – and the report is placed in the employee's file and can start the discussion at the next appraisal interview when any developments and improvements in the employee's work can be discussed. The appraisal report will usually summarise the discussion between the manager and the employee and will list any goals that were agreed, e.g. the employee might agree to try to improve their timekeeping and/or the manager might agree to find them a place on a training course. In some organisations the appraisal report will be taken into account when considering employees for promotion or salary increases.

Appraisal interviews usually take place annually but a good manager will regularly review the work of his or her staff in order to anticipate any problems. The advantage of appraisal interviewing is that it allows managers and employees to discuss, in a constructive way, any problems the employee might be having and allows the employee to put forward their ideas and suggestions. Such discussions can create a good working atmosphere thus ensuring that the organisation is working as well as possible. A disadvantage of appraisal interviews is that they are time consuming – usually involving at least half an hour – and take the manager and employee away from other work.

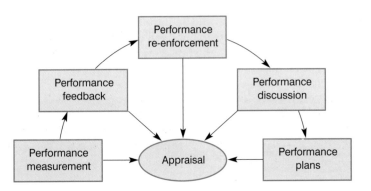

Figure 16 Appraisal should improve
performance

Letter

Letters are used by the firm to communicate with people and organisations *outside* the firm. Letters are not used for communication within the firm. The highest standards of presentation and spelling are important if a letter is to make a good impression with people outside the firm. For this reason it will be typed or word processed on high quality paper. Most firms have their name, address and logo printed at the top or bottom of the letter. It is common to have the name of the company chairman or main directors included. In a growing number of businesses e-mails will be an acceptable form of communication and letters used only for the most formal of circumstances, for example contractual or legal issues.

Memo

A memo is the form of written communication used *within* a business. Memos are not sent to people outside the organisation; a letter is used instead. A memo is used to pass on messages from one part of the business to another. This form of communication is written on a specially designed memo form. It is usually polite, brief, direct and to the point. Longer memos may have the paragraphs or each point made numbered. Memos may be typed or word processed or they may be handwritten to save time and money. In larger organisations e-mails are being used in place of memos as they are a faster method of communication.

Corporate plans

The third section of this book (page 15) describes in detail the way businesses can plan training. According to their size and culture organisations may develop an overall corporate training plan which identifies their priorities and programme for the coming period. Planning could take place at a department or divisional level, according to the size of the organisation. The plans may be communicated to employees by notices, website postings, mailings or through employee representatives. It is important for employees to understand the aims and priorities in training and other corporate plans, such as marketing, if they are to be able to focus on business priorities and take advantage of the training opportunities available.

Report

When detailed consideration of a subject, for example a proposed training event, is needed it is usual for a report to be produced. Businesses will have a house style for reports but it is common to find the following features:

- A title explaining the purpose of the report, e.g. 'A report on the impact of sales training at the Nuneaton branch during the last year'
- Results of the investigation – a straightforward factual account of the results; what the training involved and what measurable impact it had on sales; how it affected participants' perceptions and performance

- Conclusion – what the results lead you to believe; in this case whether or not, for example, the training was effective
- Recommendations – after having considered the outcomes and how the training might be changed or repeated
- Executive summary – if the person receiving the report is likely to be too busy to read it all or if the report is very long, a summary is common. The summary is a short section at the front of the report which gives brief details of the investigation, the recommendations and the reasons behind them. It sums up the report.

Notices

Notices can be an effective means of communicating non-confidential information to a large number of people. Notices should be eye-catching and convey only essential information. Notices that are too detailed are hard to read. It is good practice to make sure the notice is signed and dated by the person responsible for its display. Clear headings and pictures are effective ways of holding the readers' attention. Notices calling a meeting or training event should always have details of the date, time and place of the event and explain, briefly, the purpose of the event.

Want to know more?

Visit http://www.greatplacetowork.gov.uk/ for a number of case studies about business and communication.

Spoken communication

Spoken or verbal communication can take many forms. It may occur in an appraisal interview, passing comment, meeting, or telephone call. Spoken communication has the advantage of being fast and immediate. Feedback is almost instant when the person hears what is being said. This form of communication allows questions to be raised and answered quickly. Verbal communication speeds up the consideration of different opinions through discussion. The disadvantages of verbal communication methods are that they do not allow the same detailed level of preparation and presentation as written methods and an accurate record is hard to obtain. The telephone is important to spoken communication as it allows rapid communication over long distances. It has the disadvantage of being more expensive than most written methods of communication.

Non-verbal communication

A person's expression, the way they walk and the number of times they smile or frown give clues about how they feel. They are communicating without speaking, hence the term non-verbal communication.

The phrase body language is also used to describe this form of communication. As most body language occurs without thought it can give a clue to how a person is feeling. Care must be taken to avoid jumping to the wrong conclusions about a person. Being aware of body language can

Key term

Body language – communication occurring through sub-conscious gestures, body movement and facial expression.

help avoid being insensitive and help bring out the facts behind what others think. Watch part of a film on TV with the sound turned off. Often it is still possible to have an idea of what feelings the actors are communicating

Meetings

Meetings are a combination of verbal, non-verbal and written communication. This is because many meetings are between managers or representatives to consider reports or other written documents and to then discuss a decision. Meetings vary in size from two people to any size. Small meetings tend to be more efficient than larger ones. It is, however, important to make sure all the people who need to be involved are involved. Meetings combine the advantages of spoken communication and overcome the disadvantages of written communication. A disadvantage of meetings is that they may be used too frequently and take staff away from other work. It is a bad habit to call meetings when other forms of communication can do the job just as well. For example, it is better to write a memo than to call staff together to hear a straightforward routine announcement.

Most formal meetings have a 'chair' or 'chairperson' whose job it is to see that the meeting goes smoothly and that everyone gets a chance to contribute. The order of items to be discussed is written down in an Agenda. Someone will take a record of the meeting's decisions. The advantage of formal meetings is that they provide an accurate record of decisions and allow discussion to occur in an orderly way. They have the disadvantage of being time consuming and involve a lot of preparation and reading in advance.

Informal meetings are not as structured as formal meetings although they will have someone, such as a chairperson, to lead the discussion. They tend to be quicker and restricted to one or two particular issues. When the issues are resolved the group will stop meeting. Groups that meet on this basis are called ad hoc groups. Informal meetings have the disadvantage of often lacking formal records. The spontaneous nature of such groups may mean that certain individuals get overlooked. This can breed resentment and lead to delays.

Key term

Minutes – record of decisions taken at a meeting

ACTIVITY

Which method(s) of communication would you use to deal with these situations?
- Replying to a customer complaint
- Telling a subordinate their performance was poor
- Finding out why a delivery from an external supplier due today had not yet arrived
- Informing 10 employees that they had been accepted on the internal training course for which they had applied
- Telling staff in your department about major changes to the procedures for applying for courses and claiming associated travelling expenses where the mileage rate had been reduced.

The communication process

There are four important ingredients in the process of communication which are represented below.

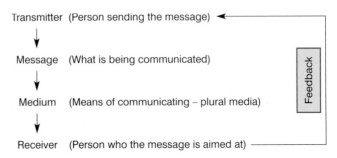

Figure 17 *The stages in the communication process*

The best sort of communication occurs when the transmitter chooses the medium appropriate to the type of message and the receiver. Sensitive information about the results of a person's examination results should not, for example, be communicated in speech over the works' loudspeaker system. A face-to-face meeting or straightforward letter is far better. An important element in communication is feedback. This is the response of the receiver to the message back to the person who sent the message. Feedback can be a letter, a shrug of the shoulders or any response to the message. Watching for feedback in communication can make the transmitter aware of the impact of the message.

There is more feedback in situations where people are encouraged to participate in decisions about their work. This two-way communication is normally found with democratic or laissez-faire style management.

One-way communication is found in autocratic styles of management. The lack of feedback in communication increases the risk that messages might be misunderstood or not even received as the transmitter gets little response to the message.

> **Key term**
>
> **Feedback** – the response of a person receiving a message to the sender or transmitter of the message.

 Democratic and laissez-faire management styles, pages 59–60

ASE STUDY

Linking Employee Attitude and Productivity

Problem/Situation

A major transportation company was interested in examining the relationship between employee attitudes and productivity. Executives were concerned about declining customer satisfaction, and wanted to examine any possible links between employee attitudes and behaviours. Once the research was completed, they expected recommendations that would result in company-wide improvements.

Methodology/Key Findings

Berrier Associates conducted a telephone survey with employees to determine employee attitudes towards their jobs and the company. Once completed, the findings were linked to specific performance measures, such as on-time delivery of shipments and percentage of damaged or lost packages. A significant link between employee attitude and performance was found.

We also found gaps between corporate communications, operational changes, and employee understanding of decisions that impacted on their day-to-day job. For example, new route planning computers given to all drivers were not being used. Employees believed they knew best how to 'run' their route and did not understand how new product categories and priorities made a 'seat of the pants' approach dysfunctional and inefficient. The company had failed to educate employees about why these computers were needed – that the new technology would ultimately improve efficiency and profitability of increasingly complex routes.

Strategy

Based on the research findings we helped implement:

- An enhanced communications strategy focused on explaining company decisions in language that resonated with employees.
- Additional training and a 'champions' program were established to improve buy-in to the operational changes.
- A corporate committee to evaluate initiatives in terms of their impact on people. Questions such as, 'Does this make sense for our workers?', 'Is there a better way to do this with less impact on individuals?', and 'Are the communications about this program adequate to answer employee questions?' are now addressed before new programs are rolled out.

Results

Productivity across the company increased, even at the worst performing locations. Employee attitudes towards their job and the company have improved, and employees are more open to change in technology and procedures.

Source: Based on research conducted by Dr Robert J. Berrier of Berrier Associates, a US based research and consulting company. Article can be found at www.berrierassociates.com

Barriers to communication

Problems, or distortion, in communication can arise for several reasons and present a barrier to effective communication.

Perceptions and attitudes

This barrier can take many forms. For example, personal stress or hostility between transmitter and receiver makes individuals less likely to share information. Possible solutions might include help or advice from colleagues or supervisors. If necessary help from a doctor or the firm's Personnel department might be needed. It is important not to 'bottle up' emotional problems or stress as this can make the problem worse.

Social differences can affect perceptions and attitudes. The supervisor might think that the new boss is 'better' than them and 'looks down' on them. This might stop them being open about problems related to the job. Insecure managers might be too formal with their staff and restrict the communication between them. These sorts of problems can only be overcome if all staff are aware of, and made secure in, their responsibility to communicate effectively. Staff training on how to work with others might ease the problem. Perceptions and attitudes will be affected by the grapevine. This refers to the informal, unofficial way information is passed through an organisation. Problems arise when there is too much unnecessary secrecy in an organisation which makes people feel suspicious and believe any information is better than no information. Poor security of confidential documents can lead to unauthorised access to information. This can feed the grapevine.

Geographical reasons

If workers are in offices throughout the world, communication is made harder because there is less feedback than in a face-to-face situation; in addition, time differences make personal contact hard to arrange. Delays in the postal service, rail strikes or motorway hold-ups can make communication difficult within a country. Even in an office, changes in the layout can make it easier for staff to contact each other and so ease communication problems. Electronic communication such as e-mail and file sharing on computer networks has helped overcome some of these problems.

Language and cultural reasons

If two people speak different languages swift effective communication will be impossible without a translator. Skills in other languages are becoming more important as the reduction in trade restrictions between European and other countries makes international trade more profitable. Language education is not sufficient unless it is linked to an understanding of other cultures. Not only do Muslim and Asian cultures, for example, represent a large part of the world economy but a significant number of successful British employees and business people have a background in these cultures. Understanding things like holidays linked to religious festivals and attitudes to criticism in different cultures are important if managers are to engage effectively with people from a variety of cultures. Even between people from the same culture using the same language, poor use of language can also be a barrier to communication. Slang, jargon and poor grammar can often serve to confuse the receiver. Training and structured overseas assignments can help to overcome language and culture problems in communication if they are clearly defined and supported.

Technical reasons

There are many examples which can be given. At a simple level the error might be to choose the wrong communication channel or medium to send a message. For example, sending an urgent letter by post when both transmitter and receiver have access to a fax machine or e-mail would be an error. Targeting the message wrongly can cause a problem. For example, not informing all of the individuals who need to know a piece of information might happen if the transmitter is unsure of a firm's structure and what the line management arrangements are. Problems of this sort can usually be overcome with good training and preparation through induction.

Principles of good communication

There are three basic principles to remember in any type of communication.

Clarity

Transmitters must be clear about what they want to say, who needs to be contacted and make sure their message is logically structured with no room for misunderstanding. Receivers must be sure they know what the message is saying and decide what it requires of them. If the receiver is unclear about what the message says or requires, this must be communicated to the transmitter, i.e. give feedback!

Concentration

Whether receiving or transmitting a message it is vital to give it your full attention. Failure to do so, in order to save a few minutes, might mean the individual spending a long time putting right an error. Examples of lack of concentration could include not writing down a telephone message because you are watching a computer screen or not checking a memo before sending it. Missing out a word like 'not' in a letter or adding a zero to a figure can have a big effect on the receiver!

Correctness

Choose the correct medium for the job and make sure the correct people receive the message. The correct medium can aid the clarity of the message; for example, a large notice with a picture might have the effect of communicating a complex idea where a long wordy memo might put readers off. There is a growing need for workers and managers alike to keep up with developments in information technology in order to use it to the full.

Want to know more?

The EU and the British government are concerned to improve
business's communication with employees as part of an effort to
increase productivity. Look at www.DTI.gov.uk for an update on the
European directive establishing a general framework for informing
and consulting employees in the European community.

National training initiatives

The object of government in peace and in war is not the glory of
rulers or of races, but the happiness of the common man.

Lord Beveridge

Many people consider the things which government does for them to
be social progress, but they consider the things government does for
others as socialism.

Earl Warren

Government, even in its best state, is but a necessary evil; in its
worst state, an intolerable one.

Thomas Paine

Since the end of the Second World War government attitudes to
training have varied between leaving market forces to work and having
highly structured industry-based plans to address skills needs.
Inconsistency has been the only consistent feature of training policy.
Between 1979 and 1997 the focus was very much on market forces. The
belief at the time was that the interaction of supply and demand would
adjust the supply of skilled employees and that wage levels would reflect
the demand for workers. Individuals, it was believed, would take up
training to exploit the available opportunities to increase their wage
levels or to end a period of unemployment. Unsurprisingly the record
numbers of unemployed people at the time, many from the efforts to
make coal, steel and shipbuilding more internationally competitive, did
not react in the way that textbook economics forecast. Unemployed
workers were reluctant to 'get on their bike' and look for work far from
where they lived in industries about which they knew little.

Improved economic circumstances in the 1990s brought about
reduced unemployment but an increased focus on skills arising through
the process of global competition. Globalisation has come to mean
increased communication, competition and interdependence of countries
in the world economy. Since 1997 the government has instituted a
number of initiatives to address the challenge of globalisation and
changes in technology. These efforts are designed to move Britain to

Key term

Globalisation – the effects of
improved transport, communications
and technology combining to
increase opportunities for the sale of
goods and services across the globe
into previously unaccessed markets.

being a high skill economy producing high value goods and services. It is argued that this is essential if the British economy is to avoid competing with its international trading partners on the basis of cheap labour producing low value items using low levels of skill.

National training initiatives since 1997 have flowed from government at a fast rate accompanied by a range of plans, strategies and targets. Government policy and supporting initiatives continue to develop at a rate that will ensure that this section of this textbook will represent only a fraction of the national initiatives and policy developments underway by the time it is published. Scrutiny of good quality newspapers, news programmes and government websites are essential to keep up to date with national training initiatives.

National training targets

Since the early 1990s governments have established a series of national training and education targets. These targets indicate the levels of education and training achievement the government believes are necessary for the UK economy to be able to compete with other countries. The targets have changed over time and new targets were established in summer 2003. Targets include the numbers of graduates to be produced, the numbers of employees achieving NVQ level 3 and two qualifications or equivalent, and targets for minimum standards of literacy and numeracy in the adult population. The purpose of target setting is to focus the minds of government departments, training providers, schools, colleges and universities on what needs to be achieved, and to measure progress. Critics of the approach maintain that targets are unrealistic and limit the ways in which organisations providing training can respond to individual needs out of fear of failing to meet their contribution to the target.

Want to know more?

Government departments particularly involved in national training initiatives include the Department for Education and Skills (DfES), Department of Trade and Industry (DTI) and the Cabinet Office. See the following websites:
www.dfes.gov.uk for the DfES,
www.dti.gov.uk for the DTI
www.cabinet-office.gov.uk for the Cabinet Office.

Investors in People (IIP)

Investors in People is a national Standard awarded to organisations, which attempts to set a level of good practice for training and development of people to achieve business goals. It is supported by a number of large national businesses, and other organisations such as the Confederation of British Industry (CBI), Trades Union Congress (TUC) and the Institute of Personnel and Development (IPD). IIP was introduced in the early 1990s and as of March 2003 a total of 33,700 organisations had achieved the standard, covering 6.9 million employees or around 28% of the workforce. A further 15,000 organisations, covering nearly 7% of the workforce, had made a public commitment to the standard, the first step in gaining recognition.

The standard provides a framework for business performance, through a planned approach to setting and communicating business objectives and developing people to meet these objectives. The aim is to match employees' skills and motivation with their employer's business interests. The Investors in People standard is based on the principles of:

- **Commitment** – a public commitment to invest in people to achieve business goals is necessary
- **Planning** – planning how skills, in individuals and teams, are to be developed to achieve these business goals
- **Action** – taking action to develop and use necessary workforce skills in a well defined and continuing programme of improvement that is directly tied to business goals
- **Evaluating** – evaluating outcomes of training and development for evidence of individuals' progress towards goals, the value achieved by training and identifying future needs.

Supporters of the standard claim that there are many business benefits arising from working towards it and achieving it. These result from the increased level of skills that meeting the standard is said to produce. The benefits are said to include:

- improved productivity and profits
- reduced costs and wastage
- improved staff motivation through greater involvement, personal development and recognition of achievement
- increased customer satisfaction – meeting the standard helps employees to effectively meet customer needs at a profit
- public recognition – this helps to attract the best quality job applicants
- providing a structured way to improve the effectiveness of training and development activities.

Want to know more?

For the full IIP standard and more details of what it involves look at http://www.iipuk.co.uk/IIP/Internet/default.htm

Critics of the IIP approach claim it only recognises what most businesses who care enough about training to seek accreditation to the standard would have done in any case. They argue that the links between improved productivity and profits and the standard are not proven or are at best overstated. Too often, it is alleged, managers are not fully committed to the standard and achieving it becomes a time-consuming 'paper exercise' carried out by the personnel or training department without any real change in business practice or links to business strategies. The purpose of the exercise is solely to achieve another award that can be displayed on company note paper and in the reception area, creating the illusion of progress to gain some publicity.

The impact of IIP is patchy although, as the case study below shows, it has the potential to benefit organisations if it is rigorously and seriously implemented. How true the criticisms of IIP prove to be will depend on the way in which firms implement it.

CASE STUDY

IT firm wins award

In January, business integration firm Sterling Commerce received the Investors in People Standard for a commitment to training. It is central to company culture, and it has become a valuable part of their rewards.

Mireille Aireault, European senior director of HR at Sterling Commerce, said: 'We offered an award to the project managers who designed the internal project management guidebook. Instead of accepting cash, they requested training. Five of them went on an Open University course.'

When training leads to higher performance, this is also recognised through reward. Aireault said: 'We recognise staff going beyond their official duties, using new skills in other arenas. A cash award of £550 was recently allocated to an employee who used their knowledge of project management methodology to organise an office move.'

Source: Based on an article at
www.employeebenefits.co.uk/News/Default.asp

 Case study: Efficient chips, page 9

Learning and Skills Council

In June 1999 the government published the 'Learning to Succeed' White Paper. This set out a vision whereby all individuals, irrespective of their background or education levels, would be given the chance to:

- learn new skills
- fulfil their potential
- improve the quality of their lives at home and at work.

Businesses, it was intended, would be able to recruit trained, talented and motivated staff in order to compete at home and abroad more effectively. The government intended that national and local skills gaps would be reduced, allowing employers to meet customer needs more effectively. In order to achieve these goals the Learning and Skills Act was passed in 2000. This created the Learning and Skills Council (LSC), which replaced the Training and Enterprise Councils (TECs).

*Figure 18 The 47 Local Learning and
Skills Councils, organised into
9 regions, attempt to help monitor
and plan local learning and
skills developments*

**Modern Apprenticeships,
pages 25 and 83**

There are 47 Local Learning and Skills Councils (LLSC) and a central
Learning and Skills Council (LSC) organisation based in Coventry,
which co-ordinates the work of the local LSCs. Together they have a
budget of around £7.3 billion and are responsible for:
- further education
- work-based training and young people
- workforce development
- adult and community learning
- information, advice and guidance for adults
- education business links.

Essentially the Learning and Skills Council is responsible for funding and
planning education and training for over 16-year-olds in England, apart
from universities. Initiatives such as Investors in People and Modern
Apprenticeships are promoted by the LSCs. They also have funds to
manage a range of projects to improve the quality of learning in colleges
and workplaces.

Critics of the LSCs point out that they are too big to be genuinely
responsive to local needs and that they impose bureaucracy on colleges
and training providers which diverts them from their core business of
delivering effective training. It is claimed that accessing funds for
training at work is unnecessarily complicated. A further criticism is that
the LSC is one of the largest publicly funded bodies in Europe but there
are no elections to any of its committees, and appointments are a
political process meaning that members of the LSC are not publicly
accountable for their actions or plans.

Want to know more?

Details of the LSC locally and nationally can be found at www.lsc.gov.uk/

Regulation of qualifications

In order to make training and learning more relevant to the needs of business and individuals the government has, since 1997, reviewed a range of qualifications. The government has introduced AS levels as the first part of the reformed A level qualification and introduced AVCEs (Advanced Certificates of Vocational Education) which it intends to be broadly similar to two full A levels. This is part of government efforts to make vocational and academic qualifications have the same standing in the eyes of the public. AS and AVCE Single awards are efforts to make the qualifications structure more flexible. The government carried out a review of the qualifications that it is prepared to fund through the Learning and Skills Council, and as a result the number of qualifications available has been reduced, although there are still nearly 90,000 recognised qualifications on the Learner Aims Database, which lists all recognised qualifications. The list is updated periodically.

The number of organisations that can award qualifications has been reduced and all qualifications now have to be approved by the QCA, the Qualifications and Curriculum Authority, before they can have national recognition. This means that awarding bodies such as AQA, Edexcel and OCR have to have their proposed qualifications approved in terms of content and methods of assessment before they can be offered to the public. These changes in the way qualifications are offered are intended to make the qualifications more consistent and easier to understand for learners, parents and employers. Critics note that this has not always been achieved and that many of the new qualifications have a complex set of administrative and assessment arrangements. Further changes are expected.

Want to know more?

For details about QCA go to http://www.qca.org.uk/about/

From the point of view of business one of the major changes of the last few years has been the introduction of National Vocational Qualifications (NVQs). There are NVQs for almost all occupations. The qualifications are offered in eleven groups:
- Tending animals, plants and land
- Extracting and providing natural resources
- Constructing
- Engineering

- Manufacturing
- Transporting
- Providing goods and services
- Providing health, social care and protective services
- Providing business services
- Communicating
- Developing and extending knowledge and skills.

The NVQ awards are offered at five levels:

- Level 1 – Foundation skills in occupations
- Level 2 – Operative or semi-skilled occupations
- Level 3 – Technician, craft, skilled and supervisory occupations
- Level 4 – Technical and junior management occupations
- Level 5 – Chartered, professional and senior management occupations.

While there is no accurate direct comparison level 2 is taken to equate to GCSE level and level 3 to A level. However, there are major differences between NVQs and these other awards.

Want to know more?

For further details on the NVQs available and how they are used in business look at http://www.dfes.gov.uk/nvq/what.shtml

 Competence based
qualifications, page 26

Key terms

Assessor – person who judges whether NVQ evidence meets the required standard and guides the learner in developing their portfolio.
Verifier – person who checks Assessment decisions. He or she may come from within the organisation (internal verifier) or outside the organisation, usually from the awarding body (external verifier).
Portfolio – collection of evidence presented by learners for assessment.

NVQs are work-related, competence-based qualifications which are intended to reflect the skills and knowledge needed to do a job effectively. They are said to represent national standards set and recognised by employers. NVQs are broken down into units which are achieved through assessment by on-the-job observation and questioning. There are no written examinations. Instead candidates have to have evidence to prove they have the competence to meet the NVQ standards. Evidence is presented in a portfolio. Assessors 'sign off' units when achieved – they test candidates' underpinning knowledge, understanding and work-based performance to make sure they can demonstrate competence in the workplace. These decisions are checked by verifiers from inside and outside the organisation.

Assessors may also work with candidates to establish what they need to do to develop the necessary skills and knowledge required by the standards and they draw up action plans with them to ensure that this is achieved.

In many businesses NVQs have been very effective in recognising what employees can do. However, it has been argued that the assessment system used for NVQs is complex and bureaucratic and that the standards are difficult to interpret. While large-scale employers have been very much involved in the development of NVQs it has been said that the standards do not fully recognise the requirements of smaller organisations where jobs and tasks are not easily defined.

Training programmes

We indicated at the start of the chapter that government from time to time involves itself in training schemes to help businesses overcome skills shortages and to help with the cost of training, while at the same time helping young people or the unemployed develop in the labour market. Two particular government training programmes are worthy of comment.

Modern Apprenticeships

From the point of view of the government the benefits of the scheme are that they provide training directly relevant to specific organisational needs. This means that even if apprentices leave an employer they will have skills that can make them employable elsewhere in the industry. Investing in this training helps businesses develop the skills to cope with new technology and new markets, often at a reduced cost.

Modern Apprenticeships, page 25

CASE STUDY

'Ours is a service and utility company that requires a very particular set of skills and there is a definite career path available. Modern Apprenticeships allow us to feed ourselves with the right people to fill the jobs we know we are going to have in three and four years time. This is definitely our preferred way of achieving this need.'

Bob Fox, Western Power

'Our Modern Apprenticeship programme allows us to develop our people; it's a good recruitment tool and a retention mechanism. We like what we've got and we're considering expanding it.'

Chris Stephenson, Egg

This means that in the longer term the Modern Apprenticeship scheme helps the government help businesses in tackling skills shortages. It is believed that the scheme helps the hundreds of participating businesses through increased staff confidence and morale. This helps with staff retention, which in turn combats skills shortages and the costs of replacing staff.

New Deal

New Deal is a broad term covering critical parts of the government's Welfare to Work strategy aimed at reducing unemployment and raising skills. Around 90,000 organisations are involved in New Deal. It gives New Deal opportunities tailored to the needs of a range of groups. These include:

- jobseekers aged 18–24 who have been claiming Jobseeker's Allowance for six months or more
- jobseekers aged 25 plus, who have been claiming Jobseeker's Allowance for 18 months or more out of the last 21 months

- jobseekers aged 50 plus who have been claiming benefits for six months or more
- jobseekers with disabilities.

Other versions of the programme include the following.

- New Deal for Lone Parents is for anyone who is looking after at least one school-aged child on their own, and claiming Income Support.
- New Deal for Disabled People is helping people on health related benefits to find work.
- New Deal for Partners. Partners of people who have been claiming benefits for six months or more can get help into work through advice, information and training.

As well as involving employers the New Deal initiative is managed through the Jobcentre Plus network of government Jobcentres.

The New Deal process starts with an interview at the local Jobcentre with a Personal Adviser who will support the New Deal participant throughout their time on New Deal. At the interview the person's skills, experience and job hopes are discussed. Any gaps in skills or knowledge are identified and the Personal Adviser may suggest extra help to get the person ready to look for work.

Various options will be considered including subsidised employment, work experience with employers, training and help with basic skills. The first part of New Deal concentrates on preparing to enter work. This is intended to ensure that employers get a recruit who is motivated and committed to the job.

If employers advertise a post as a New Deal vacancy they get a subsidy towards the wages of someone new and a contribution towards training the person for the equivalent of a day a week. More may be available if a lot of initial training is required. Employers are required to prepare an Individual Training Plan with the New Deal employee. The training will be designed to meet the needs of the employee as well as the business.

Want to know more?

For information about New Deal go to http://www.newdeal.gov.uk/

ACTIVITY

With reference to your friends and relatives, and information from government and newspaper websites, decide whether government initiatives in training are effective from the point of view of the individual, the business and the economy. Give reasons for your answers.

| Equal opportunities

Equality … is the thing. It is the only true and central premise from which constructive ideas can radiate freely and be operated without prejudice.

Mervyn Peake

Failure by an organisation to ensure that it employs and develops the best people means that it is putting itself at a competitive disadvantage. Discrimination on the grounds of race, gender and disability is not only bad business practice but morally unacceptable. By understanding the differences between employees (and potential employees) the business can identify the different potential qualities that they bring to their work. Once the diversity of the workforce, and potential workforce, is understood work, rewards and motivational methods can be tailored to meet their diverse needs and make the work more rewarding and productive. A key part of managing the diversity of the workforce is the way in which equality of opportunity for all is promoted.

Lack of opportunity commonly arises from conscious or unconscious discrimination by employers in relation to training and employment in the areas of:

- disability
- gender
- race.

Disability

The Disability Rights Commission (DRC) was established to work with disabled people and employers to ensure they are treated fairly. The DRC was set up under the Disability Discrimination Act 1995, which is intended to stop discrimination against disabled people. In relation to employment of disabled people this includes recruitment, training and benefits. The Disability Rights Commission (DRC) oversees the law and aims to, in particular:

- stop discrimination against disabled people
- promote equal opportunities for disabled people
- provide information and advice particularly to disabled people, employers and service providers
- prepare codes of practice and encourage good practice
- investigate discrimination and make sure the law is implemented.

As part of an effort to reduce discrimination against the disabled, employers should monitor the numbers of disabled people they employ and the levels they reach in the organisation and the type of work they do. In an effort to positively discriminate some employers will guarantee a job interview to those disabled people who meet the selection criteria, regardless of how many others also meet the criteria. When planning training care should be taken to ensure that facilities are accessible to the disabled in terms of ramps, hearing loops, visual enhancements and other facilities.

Disabled people who feel they have been unfairly treated can ask the DRC to investigate their case. From an employment and training point of view protection by the law does not apply to all jobs. The exceptions include:

- small businesses with fewer than 15 employees
- employment on ships, aircraft and hovercraft
- the armed services, police officers, prison officers and fire-fighting staff in fire brigades.

Want to know more?

Look at www.disability.gov.uk for information about government efforts to help disabled people.

Gender

The Sex Discrimination Acts 1975 and 1986 established that it is not legal to pay men and women different rates of pay if they are doing work of a similar nature. The law makes it illegal to treat one person more favourably than another on the grounds of their sex, not just in relation to pay but in other ways, for example promotion and training opportunities. To help prevent disputes over equal opportunities the EOC can provide advice and information to employers and employees. It provides Codes of Practice, which are guidelines for dealing with particular equal opportunities situations. Job advertisements, training and promotion opportunities can only ask for a specific gender if there is a genuine reason or genuine occupational qualification (GOC) as it is called. Acceptable reasons might include the fact that a woman is needed to supervise a residential home for the female elderly or that a man is required to model male clothes. In other words, only reasons of decency or where features typical of only one sex are required allow an employer to discriminate against one sex. It is illegal to discriminate on the grounds that customers prefer staff of one sex. For example, pubs and clubs cannot legally advertise for bar maids.

Analysing the workforce to measure the proportions of each gender in particular jobs, levels or departments is one way of ensuring that unconscious issues around gender discrimination can be addressed. Positive discrimination or affirmative action has been used by some organisations. For example, women-only courses have been used to provide a setting where women can develop their confidence and build contacts inside the organisation.

The Equal Opportunities Commission (EOC) was established under the 1975 legislation and aims to ensure that illegal discrimination is eliminated. If someone believes they have been discriminated against on the grounds of their sex they may seek help from a trade union, solicitor, Citizens Advice Bureau (CAB) or the Equal Opportunities Commission (EOC).

The EOC may, in certain circumstances, help employees who feel discriminated against to take the employer to court or an employment tribunal. An employment tribunal operates like a court and has legal powers to decide the outcome of employment-related disputes. If it suspects discrimination is taking place the EOC may issue a non-discriminatory notice against the employer. This legal document warns the employer to improve the situation or face further legal action, including fines.

Ⓒ ASE STUDY

Opportunity Now

Opportunity Now is a business-led campaign that works with employers to realise the economic potential and business benefits that women at all levels contribute to the workforce. By inspiring employers to challenge complacency and tackle barriers to women's progress, we encourage an inclusive culture in the workplace.

Since the launch of Opportunity Now in 1991 the number of participating employers has risen from 61 to 350 members among a wide range of organisations in the public, private and education sectors, establishing us as a driving force for change. Members include Abbey National plc, British Airways, BUPA, Ernst & Young, GlaxoSmithKline, HSBC Bank plc, Marks & Spencer, Morgan Stanley Dean Witter, J Sainsbury, Shell International, Tesco Stores, and Unilever UK Ltd.

The campaign is part of Business in the Community, a not-for-profit organisation representing a unique movement of companies across the UK, committed to continually improving their positive impact on society. Opportunity Now is run by a small central team based in London and a network of Regional Campaign Managers across the UK.

Source: From
http://www.opportunitynow.org.uk/case_studies_public.html

Race

The Race Relations Act 1976 made it illegal to treat one person less favourably than another in employment on the grounds of their race, nationality, colour or ethnic group. This covers all aspects of employment including training, promotion, recruitment or conditions of service. The Commission for Racial Equality (CRE) was established to ensure that the aims of the Act are met. To help prevent disputes over racial matters the CRE can provide advice and information to employers and employees. It provides Codes of Practice for dealing with particular situations where racial discrimination might occur.

One particular code of practice recommends that employers analyse the make up of the workforce to compare the ethnic distribution of employees in particular jobs, levels or departments. At a simple level one would expect the proportion of employees in the workforce from ethnic minority backgrounds to be broadly representative of the local population as a whole. Overconcentration of ethnic minorities in lower grades or low status work may be indicative of the recruitment and promotions procedure failing to account for ethnic diversity. The rates of turnover of ethnic minority staff should be similar to those from white, European descent. Analysing training opportunities and how these affect ethnic minority groups is important to ensure that access is fair. Where ethnic monitoring gives rise to concern effective training to introduce new procedures to resolve the problem may be appropriate.

Positive discrimination or affirmative action is sometimes used by employers to ensure equality of opportunity. This approach can take many forms and can include:

- targeting training at ethnic minority groups who may be under-represented due to lack of expertise but who show the potential to benefit
- training for school leavers from under-represented groups to prepare them for the available opportunities
- use of culturally sensitive materials in selection and training processes.

Practical considerations when organising training can also make a difference. For example, checking that planned events do not clash with the religious holidays of particular groups is one way. Ensuring catering takes account of those who eat Halal or Kosher food is another.

The CRE, in certain circumstances, may help employees who feel discriminated against to take the employer to court or an employment tribunal. If it suspects discrimination is taking place the CRE may issue a non-discrimination notice against the employer. This legal document warns the employer to improve the situation or face further legal action.

 **ASE STUDY**

Racism gets worse in Britain's workplaces

Racism in Britain's workplaces is intensifying as black and Asian people are now more than twice as likely to be unemployed as their white counterparts, says a new TUC report entitled *Black workers deserve better*.

Black and Asian joblessness today stands at 12 per cent, while among white people it is just 5 per cent. This position is worse than in 1990 when black and Asian unemployment was lower at 11 per cent and higher among the white population at 6 per cent. This trend has grown worse despite unemployment dropping. Black and Asian workers have clearly not gained equally from Britain's expanding economy compared to their white counterparts.

John Monks, TUC General Secretary, said: 'Too many employers are ignoring the lessons of the MacPherson Inquiry into the murder of Stephen Lawrence. They have to face up to the reality of racism in their organisations and act against it. Despite unemployment dropping below one million our black and Asian workers are still suffering discrimination.

'And this is made worse as black and Asian workers are passed over for managerial jobs, even though they have skilled themselves by gaining more higher educational qualifications. All employers should monitor their recruitment and promotion procedures and reverse this unacceptable position.'

In some of Britain's regions the situation is even worse. In both Yorkshire and Humberside and the West Midlands 5 per cent of white workers are unemployed compared to 15 per cent of black and Asian workers. But even after getting a job black and Asian workers still face discrimination as they find it increasingly difficult to get managerial posts. And this occurs despite black workers making serious efforts to equip themselves for promotion. The proportion of black and Asian workers educated to degree level or above increased from 21 per cent to 26 per cent over the last 18 months. In the same period white employees with similar qualifications only increased from 16 per cent to 17 per cent.

Source: TUC website http://www.tuc.org.uk/ 27 April 2001

Want to know more?

Look at the websites for the Equal Opportunities Commission (www.eoc.org.uk) and the Commission for Racial Equality (www.cre.gov.uk).

Discrimination

It is clear from the first part of this section that discrimination on the grounds of disability, gender or race is not only illegal but bad from a business point of view and morally indefensible. Discrimination can take several forms.

Direct discrimination

This is the obvious form of discrimination where a person is treated less favourably for training or some other aspect of employment on the grounds of their disability, gender or race.

Indirect discrimination

This is more subtle and involves using some sort of criterion that is applied equally to all but is found to be more prevalent in a particular group. For example, at one time the maximum age for entry to the Executive Grade of the Civil Service was 28 years old. By showing that this was not directly related to the needs of the post and disproportionately affected women who would be raising children during their 20s this condition was found to be discriminatory. In the case of race discrimination, requiring a high standard of written and spoken English for a labourer's job where the need for such a high standard was not proven would be another example of indirect discrimination.

Vicarious discrimination

This occurs when discrimination takes place on behalf of the owner of a business, with or without their knowledge. The fact the owner did not make the discriminatory decision but that an employee acting for the firm did so means that the owner and the business are still legally responsible. If businesses are to avoid discriminatory behaviour it is essential that managers and staff be sensitive to race, disability and gender. Training in how to make the most of the skills of all the workforce and appreciate the differences between individuals is essential therefore for business success and individual fulfilment.

Appendix: External assessment, short answer questions

Case study: Woodlands Automotive Company

Woodlands Automotive has a new company headquarters in Stockport, Cheshire on a sixty acre site. At this site five hundred people are employed. They build lorries to customer specifications. Much of the work is done on the production line and it is important that workers co-operate closely to avoid accidents. The industry is very competitive – in the 1970s there were over sixty manufacturers of lorries in Europe, now there are only 10.

Woodlands pays all of its employees annual salaries, in contrast to other organisations within the automotive industry, where some employees are paid weekly. The salaries at Woodlands are around the average for the industry and are paid on a monthly basis. Salaries are set in bands, which reflect the employees' status in the firm. Within the bands, scales are set which reflect the number of years employees have been with the firm.

Individual performance appraisal takes place annually. During the interview goals, targets and bonus pay awards are set for employees. The appraisal interview is carried out by the individual's line manager.

There is a company pension contribution scheme. Employees pay five per cent of their salary into the pension scheme and the company adds a greater percentage to it, giving a guaranteed pension upon retirement.

Weekly meetings are held with all Heads of Department to encourage co-operation between departments. All departments are interdependent and need each others' co-operation.

Promotion is from within where possible. The company occasionally allows six month transfers for people to experience the work of other departments.

Questions

1. Explain why the use of appraisal interviews is likely to be an effective method of communications for Woodlands. **(4)**
2. Herzberg described pay as a 'hygiene factor' which would remove dissatisfaction but would not create motivation. Identify two factors from the case study that would create 'motivation' according to Herzberg. Explain clearly why each would act as a 'motivator'. **(4)**
3. Appraisal interviews form an important part of assessing the training needs of employees on the production line at Woodlands, but managers also use fault analysis and observations. Explain the

relative benefits of each of these methods for assessing the
training needs of Woodlands' production line workers. (9)

4. Woodlands wish to update their operatives in Health and Safety
issues related to the organisation. Evaluate whether 'off-the-job'
or 'on-the-job' training would be more efficient for the company
and the trainees in this situation. (9)

5. To what extent would a 'laissez faire' style of management be
appropriate for the role of catering manager at Woodlands? (5)

Mark scheme

Question	Expected answers	Mark allocation
1	The need for communication, e.g., • To motivate employees • To assess training needs • To identify other problems • Assess suitability for promotion	1 mark for the reason for the communication (up to 2)
	How appraisal interviews enhance these, e.g.: • Targets are set/bonus pay award made against target or performance. • Employees can indicate their needs/Appraisal considers performance over the last year • Discussion on a one to one basis can be used to bring out any problems • Interview allows wider discussion about aspirations, etc.	1 mark for explaining how the appraisal interview achieves this (up to 2) **(4 marks)**
2	Factors: • Target setting and reward – sense of achievement • Chance of promotion – improvement and enhanced esteem • Allowing transfers to other departments – job enrichment (Do not accept hygiene factors, e.g., pensions)	1 mark for naming the factor. 1 mark for why this acts as a motivator **(4 marks)**
3	Clear indication of what each method involves, e.g.: • Appraisal interview – interactive discussion	1 mark for showing what each method involves.

Question	Expected answers	Mark allocation
3 cont.	• Fault analysis – analysis of a record of operator's errors • Observation – employees actually observed doing the job. • (These points may be made, or implied in candidates' general answers.)	
	Relative benefit of each method and how this assesses training needs, e.g.: • Appraisal allows discussion and for employees to express what they think are the important training needs, the other methods do not. • Fault analysis records actual problems over a period of time, appraisal is only occurring once a year. • Observation shows why something is going wrong and what needs to be corrected, fault analysis may only show the end result of the fault.	1 mark for each relative benefit (up to 3 marks) 1 mark for showing how each will identify training needs.
	(Note that benefit must be compared with at least one other method to be relative.)	**(9 marks)**
4	Recognition of terminologies (this may be implied)	1 mark for full recognition
	Comparative benefits of the two methods, e.g.: • With off-the-job training there will be no interruptions from their normal jobs, therefore the employees can concentrate the training. • With off-the-job training large groups can be instructed at the same time and therefore it is more cost effective. • If the new procedures refer to new equipment, etc., that is not yet installed off-the-job training may be the only method possible.	1 or 2 marks for comparative explanation of benefits (up to 6 marks) 1 or 2 marks for examples and explanations of specific situations (up to 4 marks).

Question	Expected answers	Mark allocation
4 cont.	• On-the-job training will be less disruptive to business but it may be difficult to achieve.	
	Relation of the method of training to specific situations, e.g.: • Some H & S issues relate to machinery being operated and this is best shown on-the-job. • Some H & S issues are general, e.g., evacuation procedures in the case of a fire and are best explained/practised without the distraction of work.	(N.B. a maximum of 6 marks should be given if only the business point of view is considered) **(9 marks)**
5	Understanding of term – to allow staff to make their own decisions (may be implied in the answer).	1 for understanding of the term.
	When appropriate, e.g.: • Skilled chefs deciding what/how to cook. • The order of certain basic tasks, e.g., which items to wash up first. • When duties have been delegated to assistant catering managers.	2 marks for examples of when this would be appropriate.
	When not appropriate, e.g.: • When working out rosters. • When ensuring standards of hygiene or health and safety. • When involved with hiring or firing of staff. • Deciding when meals will be served.	2 marks for when this would not be appropriate.
	(Answers should reflect 'extent' and that the management's style is both appropriate and inappropriate, depending on circumstances.)	**(5 marks)**

Index